Praise for *The Second Estate*

"The secret tax lives of the rich have long been unknowable. No more. Madoff renders her essential exposé with generosity and wit, making *The Second Estate* as enjoyable as it is devastating."

BRANKO MILANOVIC, author of *The World Under Capitalism*

"The most important book you could read this year on tax policy and reducing inequality. Readable and illuminating, Madoff explains how a tax system can protect democracy and strengthen an economy—or fuel an oligarchic upward redistribution of wealth and power."

CHUCK COLLINS, author of *Burned by Billionaires: How Concentrated Wealth and Power Are Ruining Our Lives and Planet*

"*The Second Estate* details the intricacies by which the tax code creates two tax systems: one for wage earners, one for those with financial income. Within this system, billionaires benefit from lower tax rates and tax deferrals and can even escape taxation entirely. Madoff's answer—not for the faint of heart—is to pursue the daunting challenge of tax reform, building a fairer tax system that is better suited to today's economic disparities."

KIMBERLY CLAUSING, author of *Open: The Progressive Case for Free Trade, Immigration, and Global Capital*

"No one but Ray Madoff could write a page-turner on the US tax code. *The Second Estate* is a startling exposé of how the richest

Americans are accumulating wealth in ways that are nearly, if not completely, tax-free. Madoff shows how they did it and how we got here. It's essential reading for anyone interested in the rise of economic inequality and extreme wealth."

JONATHAN LEVY, author of *Ages of American Capitalism*

"No one is happy with the US tax system. Madoff presents a clear and comprehensive look at how America's most affluent households have taken advantage—legally—of the various complexities in the tax code to shield themselves from the taxes that ordinary Americans pay. Understanding these tactics is critical to designing a better system in a world with substantial inequality and an unsustainable fiscal outlook."

WILLIAM GALE, Brookings Institution

"Madoff exposes the misalignment of the US tax code, especially how it serves the interests of the very wealthy at the expense of working Americans. A must-read for anyone seeking to understand one of the defining shortfalls of our country."

ROBERT PRICE, Price Philanthropies

THE
SECOND
ESTATE

THE SECOND ESTATE

How the Tax Code Made an American Aristocracy

RAY D. MADOFF

THE UNIVERSITY OF CHICAGO PRESS · CHICAGO

The University of Chicago Press, Chicago 60637
Published 2025
Printed in the United States of America

34 33 32 31 30 29 28 27 26 25   1 2 3 4 5

ISBN-13: 978-0-226-83520-4 (cloth)
ISBN-13: 978-0-226-83521-1 (ebook)
DOI: https://doi.org/10.7208/chicago/9780226835211.001.0001

Library of Congress Cataloging-in-Publication Data

Names: Madoff, Ray D. author
Title: The second estate : how the tax code made an American aristocracy / Ray D. Madoff.
Description: Chicago : The University of Chicago Press, 2025. | Includes bibliographical references and index.
Identifiers: LCCN 2025013854 | ISBN 9780226835204 cloth | ISBN 9780226835211 ebook
Subjects: LCSH: Taxation—United States | Tax planning—United States | Rich people—United States
Classification: LCC HJ2381 .M33 2025 | DDC 336.200973—dc23/eng/20250609
LC record available at https://lccn.loc.gov/2025013854

♾ This paper meets the requirements of ANSI/NISO Z39.48-1992 (Permanence of Paper).

Authorized Representative for EU General Product Safety Regulation (GPSR) queries: **Easy Access System Europe**—Mustamäe tee 50, 10621 Tallinn, Estonia, gpsr.requests@easproject.com
Any other queries: https://press.uchicago.edu/press/contact.html

To Dave, Gabe, Jesse, and Milly, my everythings.

The Second Estate was the official designation of the aristocracy of prerevolutionary France.

Members of the Second Estate enjoyed special privileges, including the right to hunt, carry a sword, and not pay taxes.

Contents

Preface

Every professor has an area of expertise. Mine is the tax code. For more than three decades I have taught law students the principles and subtleties of this document that does more to shape American economic life than any other. The tax code, in all its seven thousand pages of excruciating and arcane detail, directs the flow of wealth and capital in the United States.

The tax code is a set of laws, and accordingly, it is subject to amendment. For much of the twentieth century, these amendments were frequent, as Congress revised laws to account for the new and creative ways that individuals (and increasingly, their tax advisers) found to circumvent the spirit of the existing rules. This relationship between private actors and public regulation was normal, even healthy, and it produced a tax system that was continually refined to reflect the society and government that it financed.

Over the past forty years, the tax system has changed. Maintenance of the tax code has slowed, as has its enforcement. As private wealth has dramatically compounded, the redistributive promise of the tax code has been hamstrung by private interests that seek to prevent it from catching up to changes in society. The tax code has become a means for increasing concentrations of wealth as opposed to being a bulwark against it.

Today, it can be difficult to fathom how much wealth the truly wealthy have. This is complicated by the fact that words like *millionaire, billionaire,* and *trillionaire* all sound much the same, and we have so few reference points for what each means. Adding to this confusion, the word *millionaire* has traditionally been synonymous with being very rich. But today, in many parts of the country, someone with a million dollars would have a hard time maintaining what many of us have come to think of as the basics of a middle-class lifestyle, like owning a home and being able to send children to college.

Beyond the growing expenses of modern life, there is also a profound mathematical difference between a million dollars and a billion dollars. Imagine, as a thought experiment, that a millionaire tried to finance her life using only interest generated by her income (as many wealthy people endeavor to do). At a 3 percent interest rate, $1 million would return only $30,000 in income a year, barely enough to support a subsistence-level existence in most US cities. Meanwhile, $1 billion at 3 percent interest would produce an annual income of $30 million—enough to support even the most lavish lifestyle, all while preserving the principal, which could then be passed on to children, who can use the income to support *their* lifestyle.

The comedian Gary Gulman provides another way of understanding the magnitude of billions of dollars of wealth when he describes how someone could obtain the $59 billion in wealth that Bill Gates owned in 2011: "You could [achieve] it by winning the Mega Millions $100 million jackpot lottery every week for 600 weeks." "But I warn you," Gulman added, "that type of streak is very rare."[1]

Until very recently, billionaires were few and far between. The very first billionaire in the United States was John D. Rockefeller, worth about $1.4 billion (or about $30 billion in 2024 dollars) when he died in 1937. The country did not see another billionaire for fifty years, when Bill Gates achieved a net worth of $1.2 billion in 1987.

Since Gates, the billionaire class has grown exponentially, both in the number of billionaires and in the size of their wealth, which has far outpaced inflation.[2] In 2024 there were over 750 billionaires, and more than a dozen people had wealth in excess of $100 billion, including Gates, who had personal wealth in excess of $138 billion even after funding his foundation. Gates has since been far surpassed by the likes of Warren Buffett ($150 billion), Larry Ellison ($175 billion), Mark Zuckerberg ($181 billion), Jeff Bezos ($197 billion), and Elon Musk ($244 billion).[3] Given the growth rate of the wealth of the wealthiest Americans— and, as we will see, the lack of meaningful taxation of the sources of that wealth—it is only a matter of time before the US will see its first trillionaire, with others to follow.*

Meanwhile, as the United States faces a growing fiscal crisis and constant annual deficits, public conversations have rightly focused on how the federal government can close the gap between its revenue and its expenditures. A frequent refrain is that taxing the rich wouldn't make much difference in this.[4] But the top-line numbers of the federal budget show that claim to be without merit. In 2024, the country's expenses were $6.7 trillion; but the total tax revenue collected by the federal government from all sources, including corporations and individuals, was only $4.9 trillion. To cover the shortfall, the United States had to borrow an additional $1.8 trillion, adding even more to the country's mountainous national debt. In the same year, the amount of wealth owned by the wealthiest 1 percent of Americans was over $47 trillion.[5]

Some may believe that much of this $47 trillion has already been heavily taxed by the progressive income tax, or will soon be subject to estate and gift taxes, but one of the central claims of this book is that the nature of wealth has changed and grown such that our traditional tax instruments—the progressive income tax and the estate and gift tax—are not reaching the wealth where it currently

---

* The gaping divide between a million and a billion pales in comparison to the difference between a billion and a trillion. To put it in perspective, thinking on a time scale can help. Where a million seconds takes twelve days, a billion seconds takes thirty-one years; meanwhile, a trillion seconds takes 31,688 years—stretching back to a time when Neanderthals walked the earth.

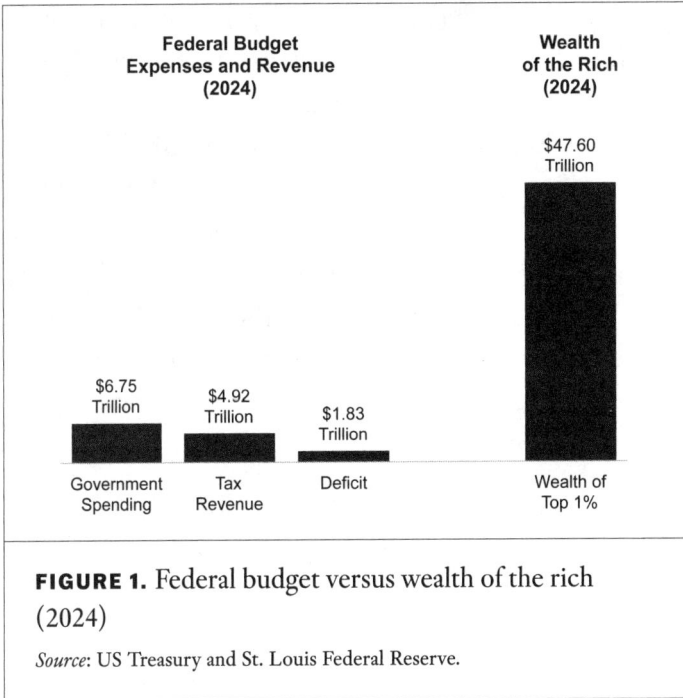

FIGURE 1. Federal budget versus wealth of the rich (2024)

Source: US Treasury and St. Louis Federal Reserve.

lives. That is not to say that a newfangled wealth tax is the answer; as this book details, such a tax would bring its own challenges. But any serious attempt to fix the concentration of wealth in the United States must begin by looking at how that concentration happened in the first place. The answer is the tax code.

This book is not the first attempt to address the tax code as a source of American inequity. It is original, however, in showing the ways the public has been deceived about who carries the costs of the federal government and the extent to which the rich are contributing to the public good. This deception has allowed the flourishing of a system in which the wealthy have been able to take advantage of—and in some cases, have exacerbated—the shortcomings of a highly imperfect American institution. Their tax strategies, coupled with narratives of wealthy benevolence and the purported hardships of being wealthy in the United States, are as much a part of the story of inequity as the tax code itself. Taken together, the result has been the creation of an entirely new class of tax-free Americans: our very own Second Estate.

1 THE PRESIDENT AND THE BILLIONAIRE

In February 2011 President Barack Obama awarded billionaire Warren Buffett the country's greatest civilian honor, the Presidential Medal of Freedom, citing Buffett's financial acumen, humility, and generosity. This kicked off an extremely public and doting period in the relationship between the president and the country's most famous investor and second-richest person. The medal was followed less than a year later by President Obama's announcement in his 2012 State of the Union address that he would pursue ambitious new tax legislation to address the country's most pressing fiscal problems and reinstate tax fairness. He called the new policy "the Buffett Rule."

Their relationship may have flourished most publicly in this period, but it was not the beginning of it. According to Obama's 2006 memoir *The Audacity of Hope*, published shortly before the launch of his first presidential campaign, his relationship with Warren Buffett began several years earlier. The book recounts Obama's visit to Buffett's office in Omaha, Nebraska, at the modest headquarters of his highly successful investment company, Berkshire Hathaway. There, Buffett laid out his complaints about the US tax code, including how it favored rich people like Buffett over regular working Americans. To illustrate his case, Buffett noted that his secretary, Debbie Bosanek, paid taxes at more than twice the rate that he did. As a working person, Bosanek was subject to both income taxes and payroll taxes; Buffett, who drew his income almost exclusively from investments, was taxed at the lower tax rates reserved for capital gains and dividends. Bemoaning the unfairness of it all, Buffett remarked, "If there's class warfare going on in America, then my class is winning."[1]

Years later, in the wake of the Great Recession, Buffett brought his lament directly to the public with an opinion piece in *The New York Times* under the provocative title "Stop Coddling the Super-Rich." Here again, Buffett outlined the specifics of his latest federal tax return, calling out how his tax rate was somewhere around half that incurred by his employees. "If you make money with money, as some of my super-rich friends do, your percentage may be a bit lower than mine. But if you earn money from a job, your percentage will surely exceed mine—most likely by a lot."[2] Here he offered a simple solution to this problem: impose a minimum 30 percent tax on all income in excess of $1 million. This, he argued, would not only reduce unfairness in the US economy; it would also stem the country's fiscal problems, including regular budgetary shortfalls and a ballooning national debt.

For Obama, the source and simplicity of Buffett's solution—not to mention the public's cheers the many times Obama brought it up in campaign speeches—made it a ready-to-wear proposal. Eager for a policy proposal with broad appeal in a reelection year, the Obama campaign brought up the Buffett Rule every chance it had. So during the 2012 State of the Union address, with Buffett's secretary Debbie Bosanek seated next to First Lady Michelle Obama, the president announced his support for the adoption of the Buffett Rule, a 30 percent tax on all income in excess of $1 million as prescribed in Buffett's *Times* opinion piece. Obama framed the Buffett Rule as a path to federal solvency, a policy that would close the country's $1 trillion deficit and "keep our investments in everything else," including "education and medical research" and "a strong military and care for our veterans."[3]

Opinion polls showed that the Buffett Rule was a huge hit with the American public, with support from 90 percent of Democrats and 53 percent of Republicans.[4] In championing the policy, Obama (like Buffett) claimed the rule offered a route to address the country's fiscal issues while ensuring that the wealthy paid their fair share of taxes.

In practice, the rule would have done neither.

That is the dirty secret of the Buffett Rule, one that Obama might easily have found out before touting it as the solution to the country's problems: For all its appearances of rigor and fairness, the rule on its own would likely have little impact on either government revenue or on the growing wealth of the richest Americans. Indeed, even Warren Buffett himself would not have paid much additional tax under the Buffett Rule.

The Buffett Rule "solution" was to impose higher tax rates on wealthy individuals who had lots of taxable income that were eligible for lower rates. But this ignored the fact that wealthy people in the US are often able to avoid taxable income altogether, which in turn allows them to avoid taxation, too. Higher tax rates matter only for those with high taxable incomes. But for many wealthy Americans, taxable income has become a matter of choice—a nonnecessity that can be avoided with little cost.

Buffett's own finances illustrate this reality. At the time of his *New York Times* op-ed, Buffett was worth over $47 billion. But his taxable income that year was only about .01 percent of that amount, because Buffett's salary from Berkshire Hathaway was relatively low for a person of his stature—$100,000 in salary and bonus, total.[5] In addition, he received no taxable returns from his ownership of Berkshire Hathaway stock, because as a matter of policy, Berkshire Hathaway doesn't issue dividends, but instead passes profits on to investors in the form of growth in the value of its stock.[6] This growth in value occurs tax-free until the stock is sold. Buffett's no-dividend policy not only saved him from substantial tax burdens; it also saved his Berkshire Hathaway shareholders from them as well.

While Buffett's comments about differing tax rates were correct—taxing income from dividends and capital gains at lower rates *does* benefit the wealthy and leave workers subject to greater tax burdens than billionaires—his solution would have done little to impose greater taxes on the rich or provide meaningful revenue to meet the country's expenses. Indeed, when it was scored by the Joint Committee on Taxation (the bean counters who measure the financial implications of proposed congressional legislation), the Buffett Rule was estimated to raise less than $47 billion *over ten years*. Considering that the deficit ran at about $1 trillion in 2012 alone, it's plain to see how the Buffett Rule was far from the panacea that Buffett and Obama suggested it could be.

At face value, the Buffett Rule failed because it wouldn't raise significant revenue in the way it promised. In a broader sense, its failure reflects a reality that, when it comes to the financial lives of wealthy people today, there's a lot more going on than Buffett or anyone else wants to acknowledge.

What neither Obama nor Buffett said—but could have to provide a fuller and more accurate description of the problem—is that the United States has allowed many of its wealthiest individuals to quietly secede from the country that benefits them financially. As the richest 1 percent of Americans have come to control more than 30 percent of the country's wealth, the tax code has given them the tools to abdicate their responsibilities and, in a sense, to relocate to a tax-free version of American life—a wealth island of sorts. While millions of working Americans (including Buffett's secretary Debbie Bosanek, as well as those earning much more) pay substantial portions of their resources to support the expenses of the country—its social safety net, national defense, interest on the national debt, and the myriad other expenses that are needed to support the most economically developed country in the world—the individuals on wealth island are insulated from such workaday burdens by a tax system that imposes little or no tax on their most common sources of wealth: investments and inheritances. Their ability to avoid taxes in those areas allows their wealth and power to grow unabated and exponentially.

The existence of these two different systems—one for people who earn money, one for people who own wealth—bears remarkable resemblance to the tax system of prerevolutionary France, in which the aristocracy was written out of the tax system, leaving the burdens of the country's expenses to everyone else. As the French economist Pierre-Samuel du Pont de Nemours (who later fled to America with his two sons, one of whom founded DuPont chemical company) said to the French National Assembly, "In order to become noble, it is sufficient to become rich; and to cease to pay taxes, it is sufficient to become noble. So there is only one way of escaping taxation, and that is to make a fortune."[7]

In France, these untaxed rich were known as the Second Estate—nobility who enjoyed sweeping financial and social privileges on the basis of their wealth. As was the case then, the existence today of a class of untaxed elites signals something broken and alarming about the US economy. It also invites the question of how a country founded on principles of equality—and with a special aversion to aristocracy—could end up where it has.

THE ACCIDENTAL TAX HAVEN

The decay of the tax code and its effects on wealth and class have been excruciatingly piecemeal, with no incident of origin or nefarious mastermind. But the timeline and scale are nonetheless quite clear.

Beginning in the early twentieth century, the American tax system was redesigned to impose its heaviest burdens on those with the greatest capacity to pay—the famed "progressive" nature of the US tax system. This marked a significant transformation from the prior system, in which the federal government raised most of its needed revenue from tariffs on imports, which consumers bore in the form of higher prices.[8]

The move away from tariffs was driven in part by a need for additional federal revenue, as the money from tariffs was no longer great enough to support the needs of a modern industrial state, or to finance the country's entrance into World War I.[9] But the choice of what to tax—including the focus on taxing the rich—was a direct response to the radical transformation in the country that had taken place since the end of the Civil War, with the transition from an economy that was broadly agrarian and largely equal (at least for white men) to one that was highly industrialized and characterized by extreme inequality.[10] Those who benefited from industrialization acquired massive amounts of wealth and were in the process of passing on that wealth (and power) to their heirs, who in turn began displaying all the trappings of the European monarchy—the exact class behaviors that American culture had rejected. At the same time, many working Americans experienced extreme financial vulnerability, beholden to the whims of the rich for their livelihoods. The increasing disaffection of this working class caused many to worry that the country would abandon capitalism and succumb to growing socialist movements.

In response to these pressures, a new ethos for taxes took hold: Taxes should be imposed on the basis of means, with the greatest burden falling to those with the greatest capacity to pay. The same principle remains alive today, at least in spirit, as evidenced by the fact that Warren Buffett's account of his secretary's higher tax rate was such an effective rallying cry. Such "tax the rich" sentiments informed the design of the two tax rules at the core of the modern tax system: the income tax, adopted in 1913, and the estate tax, adopted three years later, in 1916. These two taxes originally applied to only the wealthiest Americans, leaving more than 95 percent of Americans unaffected. But even when the income tax system was expanded to apply more broadly in order to fund World War II (which is sometimes described as moving it from a class tax to a mass tax), the focus on the rich was maintained by having a rate structure that imposed higher tax rates on those with greater income. And the estate tax was imposed at increasingly higher rates.[11]

Though far from perfect, these rules generally worked, at least through the 1970s. They imposed significant taxes on the wealthy, and they generated sufficient revenue to pay the country's expenses, including funds for several major wars as well as for social programs that provided housing and education, which in turn built a strong middle class.

The situation changed in the 1980s as wealth began concentrating among the richest Americans, eventually reaching levels not seen since the Gilded Age of the early twentieth century.[12] Meanwhile, since 2001, the federal government has faced shortfalls in tax revenue that have left the country unable to pay for its most basic expenses.[13] As a result, the country has accumulated a staggering debt. In 2024 this debt required the federal government to pay more in interest than it paid for national defense.[14]

So what changed? Today's income tax and estate tax take the same forms, and appear to serve the same goals, as the rules adopted over a century ago. The income tax still has progressive tax rates, meaning they are higher for people with more taxable income and exempt many lower-income Americans altogether. The estate tax is designed to impose a separate tax on the richest Americans as they pass their wealth to the next generation. Yet evidence shows that these taxes are not doing what they purport to do.

The income tax is still formally structured to take the most from people who can most afford it, but its capacity to do so has been undermined by wealthy people's avoidance of taxable income. Economists and tax experts have long recognized the ability of the wealthy to avoid taxable income, but with secrecy around tax returns, it was difficult to uncover real-world examples. This all changed in June

2021, when journalists at ProPublica published a series of articles based on actual tax returns leaked by an Internal Revenue Service (IRS) contractor (his name: Charles Littlejohn, like the *Robin Hood* character). The returns showed that many of the country's richest Americans—with household names like Michael Bloomberg, Elon Musk, Jeff Bezos, George Soros, and even Warren Buffett—had all largely avoided income taxes by avoiding taxable income. In some cases, these billionaires paid no income taxes at all despite their shared status as some of the wealthiest people in the world.[15]

The other plank of the tax code, the estate tax and gift tax (along with the generation-skipping transfer tax, adopted to fortify the estate and gift tax in 1986), was explicitly designed as a bulwark against large intergenerational transmissions of wealth. Complementing the income tax, the estate and gift taxes promised to preserve an egalitarian American society—and for many decades they *did*. But the estate tax, like the income tax, is no longer doing what it was designed to do. While there is no Charles Littlejohn–style cache of elite tax returns to substantiate how the tax isn't working, the American economy itself provides the proof. Concentrations of wealth have moved from historic lows in the 1970s to heights not seen since before the advent of the modern US tax code. And while the richest Americans control more wealth than ever, the amount of money raised by the estate and gift tax—which supposedly apply broadly to all wealth transfers at death and also during life—is minuscule, providing less than one-half of

1 percent of total federal revenue. Meanwhile, a full 33 percent of Americans on the list of four hundred richest families are there by virtue of inherited wealth.[16] The channels to avoid the estate tax are not just well known; they are thriving, and the result has been the safe passage of wealth within families across decades.

The failure of the income and estate taxes to keep up with the flows of wealth has produced a natural refrain: "Create new taxes geared specifically to growing wealth." This is a well-intentioned argument. But it is more challenging to implement than it appears.

THE WEALTH TAX GAMBIT

Given the booming amount of wealth held by relatively few people in the United States, it's little wonder that many politicians have shifted their sights to imposing annual taxes on wealth—either on total wealth or on growth in wealth—as a way of increasing federal revenue. While such taxes have the promise of generating significant tax revenue, and in turn of limiting the wealth of the richest Americans, there are reasons to be pessimistic about their viability.

First, taxing wealth could be found unconstitutional by the Supreme Court, particularly in light of the 2024 Supreme Court case *Moore v. United States*.[17] The *Moore* case centered on a very narrow issue of law involving an obscure tax on foreign income, but the case was funded by antitax advocates who hoped the outcome of the Court's decision would be to render all wealth taxes unconstitutional, forever. In its opinion, the Court ultimately sidestepped the broader issue but left the constitutional issue open for another day. Several justices seemed open to a broader application of the ruling, so many legal experts remain pessimistic that wealth taxes would survive constitutional scrutiny in the future.

There are other practical reasons to question the viability of annual taxes on wealth, too. Taxes on wealth, or on growing wealth, require taxpayers to regularly report everything they own and its value. This type of reporting requirement would likely feel highly intrusive to Americans who are used to keeping their wealth private, and they would be well positioned to make a case for their privacy in court.

There is also the question of how one sets an annual value on an asset, particularly assets like privately held business interests, collectibles, or really anything other than a publicly traded stock. Imagine everything of value in your life. Now imagine documenting the value of each of those things once a year, every year. The difficulty of this task would be eclipsed only by the challenges the IRS would face in policing such an undertaking, particularly as taxpayers and their advisers would have ample incentive to create complex structures to hide the true value of their assets. While this tallying is currently required after death for those who are subject to the estate tax, it is a onetime calculation made in connection with transferring wealth from one owner to another. It is far less intrusive than the annual calculations and disclosures that would be required by annual wealth taxes.

Finally, and most significantly, taxes on wealth may create serious unintended consequences, including a negative financial impact on the many Americans who invest in the stock market, either directly or through their retirement accounts. The ease of valuing publicly traded securities may cause wealthy taxpayers to move their funds out of publicly traded stocks and into privately held business interests, art, and collectibles, all of which are much more difficult for the IRS to value. If this were to happen on a large scale, the movement away from the stock market could reduce the value of the stock market as a whole, with drastic financial repercussions for the US, its residents, and the global financial system.

The wealth tax continues to be promoted by some politicians and prominent economists.[18] But given the deep pockets of those who would oppose wealth taxes, along with the logistic and legal obstacles to imposing them, the adoption of a wealth tax in the US would be no small challenge. That is not to say it won't happen. But in the meantime, without it, America's broken system rattles on with an ever-increasing national debt to show for it.

HOW THE TAX-AVOIDANCE MACHINE WORKS

The tax life of America's rich is, by nature, unique to each individual. But a few core themes have emerged in the new school of tax avoidance and the building of dynastic wealth—that is, wealth passed down through families. The following main themes, along with a discussion of their origins, implications, and possible remedies, are the focus of this book (of course, there's lots more, too, so read on!).

Rich People Avoid Income Taxes by Avoiding Taxable Income

Most Americans depend on heavily taxed earnings from work to support themselves and their families. Meanwhile, many of the richest Americans avoid taxes by avoiding salaries—with many like Larry Ellison (Oracle) and Mark Zuckerberg (Meta) having taken $1 a year, while others, like Elon Musk (Tesla), have taken zero, causing the State of California, for example, to charge Tesla with violating its minimum-wage laws.[19] Importantly, these individuals are not eschewing financial gains from their businesses altogether. Instead, they are counting on the growing value of their stock holdings to build their wealth. Relying on growth instead of income helps them avoid significant taxes because that growth is not subject to tax until and unless they sell the stock. And if they hold it until their death, all the gains are washed away, never to be taxed. Then, their heirs are treated as if they bought the stock at market value, so they don't pay taxes on any of the deceased's gains, either. Meanwhile, the wealthy can access their wealth to support their lifestyle through tax-free borrowing against their assets.

The ability to avoid taxable income is not limited to billionaire entrepreneurs. Many "regular" rich people can also enjoy the benefits of borrowing tax-free against their growing investments instead of selling their stock or receiving dividends. What *is* relatively new, though, is the widespread reliance on increases in stock value, as opposed to salary or dividends, as a means of acquiring wealth. Before 1982, this path was not generally available, because corporations typically shared profits by paying salaries to top executives and other workers, and dividends to shareholders. Both salaries and dividends were generally subject to tax at the highest rates.[20] However, after 1982, due to a change in Securities and Exchange Commission (SEC) rules that allowed stock buybacks, many companies stopped using profits to pay dividends and instead used them to purchase their own stock on the open market (called *stock buybacks*), which had the effect of raising the value of their stock. This shift from dividends to stock buybacks had an extraordinary effect on the market, boosting the prices of stocks to unprecedented levels. It also eliminated a significant source of tax revenue (taxes on earnings and stock dividends) and gave wealthy investors an easy way to grow their wealth tax-free.

Working People, Especially Working Rich People,
Pay for the Country's Biggest Expenses

The country's biggest expenses by far are its social insurance programs: Social Security and Medicare, unemployment insurance, and other social insurance programs. These programs account for more than half the country's expenses and, as the result of an aging population and a decrease in the ratio of workers to retirees, face fiscal hardship.

The richest Americans pay hardly anything in support of these programs, because the programs are largely funded through payroll taxes imposed on earnings. By avoiding earnings, the rich avoid payroll taxes as well.

Meanwhile, in terms of raw volume of taxes being paid, no group pays more than the working rich of the United States—the people working high-paying jobs (and thus paying high income taxes on top of payroll taxes) and not benefiting from the tax-avoidance devices of those wealth owners who can afford to live without salaries. This amounts to a crucial difference between America's working rich and its plutocratic rich: The former work and have to pay taxes; the latter might work but have the means to circumnavigate the system to avoid paying taxes in ways the working rich can't.

The Estate Tax Is Effectively Dead (and Should Be Laid to Rest)

Although the estate tax still officially exists, its efficacy and the public perception of it was severely damaged as part of a 1990s public relations campaign to portray the estate tax— a tax paid on inherited wealth over a certain threshold—as a "death tax" and "an unfair double tax that hurt family farms and businesses." The campaign, financed by some of America's wealthiest families, achieved only limited success in its goal of repealing the estate tax altogether—they managed a one-year suspension, in 2010—but its more fundamental success was turning the public against the estate tax. Since then, public antipathy, along with pressure from rich donors, has deterred lawmakers from doing basic upkeep to close the tax's loopholes. Indeed, since 1990, Congress has not taken a single step to close any loopholes in the estate tax. As a result, the tax stands in name only, and wealthy Americans and their financial planners avoid taxes through a virtual alphabet soup of loopholes—names like SLATs, SLANTs, GRATs and GRUTs, CRATs and CRUTs, QTIPs and QPRTs and NIMCRUTs and Flip CRUTs.[21]

Meanwhile, the US income tax system—developed on the assumption of a well-operating estate and gift tax—continues to impose no income taxes on people who receive gifts, inheritances, or life insurance distributions, no matter how large. As a result, someone who receives a $10 million gift or inheritance is treated the same, taxwise, as a person who has no income at all.

Philanthropy Is a Rich Person's Game, and the Public Often Loses

The rich are frequently celebrated for their charitable largesse, but their philanthropy often imposes significant costs on the federal government in terms of forgone revenue, and it often provides uncertain benefits to the public.

People who work for their money receive few, if any, tax benefits from charitable giving, despite most people's assumptions to the contrary. Indeed, 90 percent of Americans get no tax benefits for their charitable donations. In contrast, those with wealth who plan their philanthropic gifts well—as most wealthy people do—can save on income taxes, capital gains taxes, and estate and gift taxes by making charitable donations of appreciated property, including stocks, real estate, cryptocurrency, and other property interests that have gone up in value. Taken together, these tax savings can save the donor, and thereby *cost* the federal government in forgone revenue, as much as 74 percent of the value of the donation. This makes American taxpayers, who must cover this forgone revenue, the unwitting and principal funders of the philanthropy of the very rich.

While some donations provide benefits to the public, there is no certainty that this will be the case. The reason is that the wealthiest Americans frequently donate their money—not to food banks or homeless shelters (or even already-rich alma maters)—but to their own private family foundations or donor-advised funds. These charitable intermediaries provide wealthy donors all the immediate tax benefits of charitable giving without imposing any time frame for the funds to be spent toward charitable ends. As a result, there is no certainty that the public will ever benefit from the donations.

Misinformation (and Partial Information) Perpetuates an Unfair System

The American tax system is allegedly progressive, but seen in the full context of today's economy, it is in fact highly regressive. This system has been allowed to flourish by a combination of two factors: the intimidating nature of the tax code, which deters people from gaining their own firsthand knowledge of the rules, and a disinformation campaign—led in part by think tanks funded by the wealthy—that was designed to mislead the public about who actually carries the costs of running the country.

After the US Constitution, the tax code is the single most important document affecting Americans' lives. But because it is a deeply opaque, seven-thousand-page document, few Americans have any idea what the code says.

Into that confusion enter people who benefit from the status quo and spread false narratives to maintain it. These actors are not just billionaires. Politicians—including presidents and presidential candidates—also carry water for the cause of the tax interests of the megawealthy.

A frequent refrain of those defending the status quo is that the income tax system already heavily burdens the rich because the top 1 percent of earners pay 40 percent of all income taxes while 40 percent of Americans pay no income taxes at all. This is partially true: Individuals with the most taxable income do pay the most income tax. However, this statistic is about people who have high incomes, typically from work; it tells us nothing about the tax liability of those with the most wealth. Studies have shown that there is only about a 50 percent overlap between America's wealthiest people and those who earn the most income.[22] Moreover, as the leaked tax returns of several of the wealthiest Americans reveal, the ability of wealth owners to avoid taxable income means that they are just as likely to be among the 40 percent of nonpayers as they are the top 1 percent of earners.

WHY THIS MATTERS

The future of the United States and its economy depends on decisions the country makes today about taxing the rich. At the time of this writing, a set of Americans who control over 30 percent of the country's wealth are under no certain obligation to support the costs of running the country. This is plainly unsustainable, and the history of political arrangements such as the Second Estate prove that they do not age well.

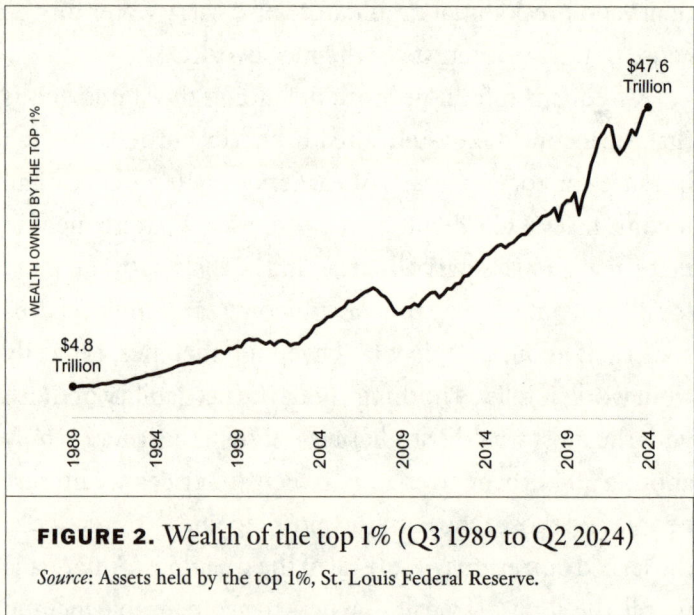

FIGURE 2. Wealth of the top 1% (Q3 1989 to Q2 2024)
Source: Assets held by the top 1%, St. Louis Federal Reserve.

Separate from the question of how to share the costs of government fairly, the failure to tax the rich also allows for that wealth to grow at warp speed, producing ever-greater concentrations of wealth. As others have noted, extreme concentrations of wealth threaten the continuing existence of the American democracy. This is not only because wealth confers power—over companies, the media, philanthropy, and politics—but also because democracy demands that elites and regular people are united in the shared endeavor of a democratic republic.[23] This is an issue not just for Democrats or Republicans, but for all Americans. What follows is designed to provide a foundation for this critical national conversation.

2 THE TAX-AVOIDANCE PLAYBOOK

During the late 1970s, Steve Martin was the most popular comedian in the United States, regularly performing in front of sold-out crowds in the country's largest arenas. His comedy was revelatory not only for its odd mix of warmth and absurdity, but for its subversion of the traditional stand-up form. "What if there were no punch lines?" Martin wrote in his memoir, *Born Standing Up*. "What if I created tension and never released it? What would the audience do with all that tension?"

In one of his most famous routines, Martin turned his attention to taxes. In the voice of a pitchman speaking directly to the audience, Martin loudly announced: "*You* can be a millionaire and *never* pay taxes! *You* can be a millionaire and *never* pay taxes! You say, 'Steve, how can *I* be a millionaire and *never* pay taxes?' First, get a million dollars. Now, you say, 'Steve, what do I say to the tax man when he comes to my door and says, "*You* have *never* paid taxes"?' *Two* simple words. Two simple words in the English language: 'I forgot!'"

The joke was extremely popular, so much so that Martin chose it to open one of his many high-profile appearances on Johnny Carson's *The Tonight Show*. One reason it consistently landed so well was that in the 1970s—with taxes imposed at historically high rates and payments enforced by a well-funded Internal Revenue Service—the idea of a rich person not paying taxes truly seemed absurd.[1]

Yet today, the joke feels almost nonsensical. Not only has the idea of a rich person not paying taxes ceased to be absurd; it's expected.

While many Americans understand that rich people often don't pay taxes, what they understand less well is how they manage to do so. This is particularly vexing because, for the vast majority of Americans, taxes are both burdensome and unavoidable.

So, how are the rich able to easily accomplish what so many other Americans can't? In the simplest terms, it's because the tax code allows for different treatment for different types of income—earnings, investments, and inheritances. The wealthy can exploit those differences in treatment to their advantage. To do so, they follow a set of strategies that limit, and in some cases altogether eliminate, their exposure to federal taxation. These strategies make up what I'll call the Tax-Avoidance Playbook, and they involve three broad tactics: avoid salaries; invest and hold investments until death (while borrowing against them as necessary for cash), a strategy called *buy, borrow, die*; and inherit wealth. For Americans with means, these three strategies have increasingly shielded them from the taxes that are, for most Americans, a necessary fact of life. What follows is a brief discussion of each strategy and its nuances.

STRATEGY 1: AVOID SALARIES

The US tax code imposes its greatest burden on people who work for their income—dishwashers and carpenters, teachers and firefighters, doctors and lawyers, corporate executives and professional athletes, and everyone in between. For everyone but the lowest earners, taxes are inevitable and meaningful. They are imposed on the first dollar earned, and after that at increasing rates.[2] Because salaries are so heavily taxed, the first play in the Tax-Avoidance Playbook is for the rich to avoid those traditional earnings. This is what many of the richest people do, particularly those whose wealth arises from their business interests, like Jeff Bezos, Elon Musk, and Warren Buffett. In general, people with high salaries pay lots of tax. Thus, people who don't need salaries avoid them, and they benefit financially from doing so.

High taxes on salaries stand in sharp contrast to the treatment of profits from the sale of investments, such as stock, real estate, art, collectibles, and cryptocurrency. The profit that results from the sale of any of these assets is called a *capital gain*, and capital gains are taxed at much

TABLE 1

A quick guide to common taxes of the United States

Type	Rate	What it applies to	What it doesn't apply to
Ordinary income tax	10%–37%, depending on taxpayer income	Earnings Interest Rent Lottery winnings All other income except capital gains	Gifts Inheritances Life insurance
Capital gains tax	0%, 15%, or 20%, depending on taxpayer income	Profits from the sale of investments	Unrealized (i.e., unsold) gains
Payroll tax	15.3% flat rate, half paid by employee and half paid by employer; self-employed taxpayers pay entirety	Earnings Self-employment income	The 12.4% tax for Social Security only applies to the first $176,100 of earnings
Estate and gift tax	40% flat rate on gifts and estates of $13.6 million or more	Property owned at death Gifts made during life	Transfers to spouses Transfers to charity Gifts for education or medical expenses Any other gifts of $18,000 or less each year

lower rates than earnings from work. Because of this difference in tax treatment, someone who earns $50,000 from working a job pays higher taxes than someone who makes $50,000 from selling an investment.

A History of Disagreements About Taxing Salaries Versus Taxing Investments

People have long held differing views about the appropriateness of the differential treatment of salaries and investments: Some see the lower tax on investment income as a natural and appropriate way of encouraging savings and risk taking; others see it negatively—as a way of providing disproportionate benefits to those who are already in a privileged position.[3]

Amid that long-standing tension, some have argued that in the interest of fairness, all income should be taxed the same, regardless of whether it comes from earnings or investments. Such was the view of Ronald Reagan, who in his signature tax bill, the Tax Reform Act of 1986, increased taxes on investment income and reduced taxes on earnings so that both would be subject to the same tax rate.[4] This was the rule from 1988 to 1990, when President George H. W. Bush raised the tax rate on income from earnings, re-creating the two-tiered system that continues to this day.[5]

Still others have argued that, out of deference to the greater vulnerability of workers, earnings from work should be taxed at lower rates than investment income. One surprising supporter of this view was Andrew Mellon, a well-known robber baron during the Industrial Revolution. Mellon, one of the richest men in America at the time of his death in 1937, was also deeply involved in matters of tax policy. He served as Treasury secretary under the presidents Warren G. Harding, Calvin Coolidge, and Herbert Hoover, and he became known for his opposition to estate taxes and other high taxes on the wealthy.

Despite these views, Mellon also believed that wages should be taxed at lower rates than income from investments. As he wrote in his 1924 book, *Taxation: The People's Business*, "The fairness of taxing more lightly income from wages, salaries or from investments is beyond question. In the first case, the income is uncertain and limited in duration; sickness or death destroys it and old age diminishes it; in the other, the source of income continues; the income may be disposed of during a man's life and it descends to his heirs."[6]

Taxes on Earnings Aren't Just Income Taxes

One reason taxes on earnings are so burdensome is that the federal government taxes earnings in more than one way. People who work—either for themselves or for others—are subject to both income taxes and payroll taxes.

Income taxes are imposed on earnings of all types, including wages, salaries, tips, bonuses, and commissions. Tax rates on this kind of ordinary income can go as high as 37 percent. Even barter is taxed: If a plumber installs a sink for a web designer, who in exchange sets up a website for the plumber, both the plumber and the web designer are expected to pay income taxes on the value of the services received.[7] The jobless are subject to taxes on their unemployment benefits; retirees are taxed on their retirement benefits; the disabled are taxed on their disability payments. Income taxes also apply to those who earn their income through a combination of work and luck, like winnings from gambling or the lottery. Even someone who finds property or money on the street is technically subject to income tax on the value of the found property.

Earnings are also subject to payroll taxes, which fund Social Security and Medicare. These taxes are often referred to as "hidden taxes," because their burden is largely hidden from taxpayers' view. Payroll taxes are usually deducted on employees' behalf and submitted to the government without the employees ever having to file a tax return, and often segregated on employee pay stubs under the mysterious term *FICA* (for Federal Insurance Contributions Act), making it difficult for individuals to see the specifics of their full tax burden.

Confusion about the nature of these payroll taxes is typical—and understandable because pay stubs and tax forms list payroll taxes as "contributions" rather than taxes, suggesting that they are somehow voluntary in nature or are set aside for the individual's personal use later on. But neither of those things is true. Payroll taxes, like other taxes, are funds that the government collects from individuals involuntarily to pay for current government expenses—in this case, Social Security and Medicare for current beneficiaries. And although paying payroll taxes establishes one's eligibility for the Social Security program, an individual has no guarantee of any particular future payment, as the program can always be altered (or even eliminated).

To be subject to these rules, and to be confused by them, is something close to a universal experience for people who earn their money from work. To quote Rachel on an episode of the sitcom *Friends*: "Who's FICA? Why's he getting all my money?"

Although payroll taxes are hidden, their burden is significant, particularly on those who can least afford them. Income taxes are imposed only after reaching a set minimum—an individual needs to earn $15,000 before owing federal income tax—but payroll taxes are imposed on the first dollar earned. In addition, while other tax rates have been significantly reduced over the past fifty years (the top income tax rate has fallen from 70 percent to 37 percent, and the top estate and gift tax rate has fallen from 77 percent to 40 percent), payroll taxes imposed on working Americans have significantly *increased*, with rates more than doubling from 7.5 percent in 1972 to 15.3 percent in 2024. So, a self-employed person who earned $15,000 in 2024 would be spared paying income tax because of low income—but would still have to pay just under $2,300 in payroll taxes.[8] Also, unlike other forms of taxation, including income and estate and gift taxes, payroll taxes do not allow any deductions for charitable donations or other expenditures.

The combination of income and payroll taxes is particularly burdensome for low- and middle-income Americans, many of whom are already struggling to get by. A self-employed mechanic who earns $60,000 (the median salary for all Americans in 2024) would pay more than $13,800 in income and payroll taxes.* For a person trying to get by on a $60,000 salary, $13,800 amounts to a massive financial hit: It could easily be the difference between whether, say, the mechanic can afford to own a car or—even more troubling—will keep or lose his housing.

Avoiding Taxes by Avoiding Compensation

Because the most common way to receive money is a salary, and because a salary is the most common way to have to pay taxes to the federal government, very wealthy people have discovered that avoiding a salary is also very helpful in avoiding taxes.

Warren Buffett keeps his salary and bonus to no more than $100,000 a year, a pittance compared to his net worth; other megawealthy individuals take an even lower salary. Indeed, taking low salaries has become de rigueur among the billionaire set. Jeff Bezos at one time earned a salary of just under $82,000 a year, low enough to make him eligible to claim the Child Tax Credit (which he did). Mark

---

* While income taxes on $60,000 in 2024 would only be $4,677, payroll taxes would be $9,180 (15.3 percent of $60,000), for a total tax liability of $13,857.

Zuckerberg is the lowest-paid employee at Meta, earning a base salary of just $1 per year.[9] Other $1-a-year billionaires include Google cofounders Larry Page (net worth $132 billion) and Sergey Brin (net worth $127 billion).

But these billionaires are not just forgoing the unfathomable compensation one would expect for being leaders of the world's most successful companies. Instead, they are well compensated through their stock ownership in their respective companies: Berkshire Hathaway, Amazon, Meta, and Google. To get a sense of the magnitude of their compensation, in just the first six months of 2023, Zuckerberg's personal wealth from his ownership of Meta increased by $58.9 billion. That is modest in comparison to Elon Musk, whose wealth grew over the same period by more than $96 billion.

The effect of forgoing a salary in exchange for company shares is not only lucrative on its own; it moves these executives from having to play by the ordinary income and payroll tax rules, which are applied to earners, to getting to play by the capital gains rules, which are applied to investments. Capital gains taxes are imposed at lower rates and are far easier to avoid, in ways discussed later in this chapter.

Like Income but Different; or, Working in Private Equity

Another way that the richest Americans avoid earnings is by claiming that their earnings from work are investment income, and thereby eligible for capital gains tax rates. This is the play of managers in private equity, venture capital, and hedge funds, who are compensated in part with a share of their fund's profits (typically 20 percent), called *carried interest*. Carried interest constitutes the vast majority of income for these fund managers. According to a 2019 survey, carried interest accounted for at least 84 percent of private equity partner compensation, with larger firms boasting figures closer to 90 percent.[10]

Carried interest is tremendously lucrative. As *Forbes* reported, "The largest paychecks on Wall Street aren't being collected in corner offices at Goldman Sachs or JPMorgan, but at the top ranks of the world's largest private equity firms, where hundreds of millions of dollars are flowing in carried interest payouts and bonuses."[11] The CEO of Blackstone, Stephen Schwarzman, is one of the most successful hedge fund managers and took home compensation in excess of $1.2 billion in 2022.[12] This eye-popping figure was eclipsed one year later by the hedge fund Citadel's CEO Ken Griffin, whose 2023 earnings of $4.2 billion made him the highest earner in Illinois. With earnings like that, Griffin had no problem spending $54 million to defeat a legislative proposal that would have raised taxes on extremely high-income Illinois residents in 2020. After defeating the proposal, Griffin still moved himself and his business to tax-free Florida in 2022.[13]

Given these eye-popping distributions from private equity, hedge funds, and venture capital, it is not surprising that many of these fund managers have become wildly rich. Indeed, their wealth is so great that *Forbes* began supplementing its traditional list of the wealthiest people with a separate report on the twenty richest hedge fund managers. All the hedge fund managers had assets in excess of $1 billion,[14] and more than sixty members of *Forbes's* "400 Richest People" list in 2023 had close ties to private equity, venture capital, or hedge fund management. These individuals had an average net worth of about $7.6 billion and combined wealth of over $465 billion.[15]

On top of these extraordinary payouts, these fund managers are able to gain even more benefits by taking advantage of the *carried-interest loophole*. Under current rules, carried interest is taxed as if it were a return on a capital investment, even though no investment of capital is made by the fund manager. As a return on investment, carried interest gets taxed at capital gains rates, which top out at a 20 percent, as opposed to the 37 percent top tax rate applicable to earnings.[16] To put this 20 percent rate in perspective, it is less than the income tax rate imposed on individuals earning as little as $48,000.[17] In addition, because carried interest is treated as a return on investment rather than earnings, it is not subject to payroll taxes.

The carried-interest loophole was first brought to national attention in 2006 by the law professor Victor Fleischer, and in the years that followed—in a rare confluence of bipartisan agreement—Presidents Obama, Trump, and Biden all issued proposals to close it. To date, no meaningful reform has been adopted.[18]

One reason is the fierce opposition to reform from lobbying groups and industry figures. Schwarzman, the Blackstone CEO with a net worth of $42 billion, was reported to have described Obama's efforts to close the loophole as "like when Hitler invaded Poland."[19] Since 2019, Blackstone has been the single largest contributor to Arizona Senator Kyrsten Sinema's political campaigns, donating more than $430,000 (alongside nearly $3 million more in funding to Sinema from other investment groups). This money was well spent, as in 2022, Sinema was credited with strong-arming Senate Democrats to drop carried-interest reform by threatening to withhold her support from their spending bill.[20]

Reform remains politically difficult, but the solution to the loophole is not itself complex: Carried interest can simply be classified as wages subject to normal income tax rules, as in the 2024 Senate bill called the Carried Interest Fairness Act of 2024.[21] Even more simply, the carried-interest loophole could be closed by reinstating the Reagan-era rule taxing all income—regardless of whether it is from investments or earnings—at the same tax rate. As of the writing of this book, neither appears politically imminent.

STRATEGY 2: BUY, BORROW, DIE

The second play used by the rich to avoid taxes is to acquire investment properties such as stocks, cryptocurrency, real estate, art, collectibles. These investments are often rewarded with higher returns in the market because they are riskier than investments in traditional savings vehicles, like savings accounts and money market funds. For those who are wealthy enough to tolerate the inherent risk of these investments, the tax code provides the benefit of capital gains treatment. Earnings from the sale of investments—that is, capital gains—are taxed at much lower rates than ordinary income. But the tax benefits of investment properties go beyond capital gains rates.

Investments can also be used as collateral for tax-free loans from banks, which means they can provide liquidity to support their owner's lifestyle without requiring that they be sold. (This is the *borrow* in *buy, borrow, die.*) But the ultimate benefit is what happens when people continue to hold their investments until death; when those investments pass to their heirs, their tax basis (the amount against which gains and losses are measured) is reset to the property's fair market value at the time of death. So, neither the decedent nor the heirs pay any taxes on investment gains that occurred before death.

The combined effect of these three rules—lower tax rates on investments, the allowance of indefinite deferral, and resetting gains to zero at time of owner's death—is that taxes on these investments are not just less burdensome but effectively optional.

Prowling for Lower Tax Rates

The most obvious benefit of paying capital gains taxes rather than income taxes is that capital gains are taxed at lower rates than salaries and other forms of ordinary income. Where those earning salaries pay income taxes at rates up to 37 percent (with additional payroll taxes of up to 15.3 percent!), capital gains rates top out at 20 percent. The stakes of this difference can be seen by considering the financial takeaways of two people who are financially involved with Uber, one as a driver and one as a shareholder. If an Uber driver earns $100,000 from driving for the platform for a year, the driver is subject to income taxes and payroll taxes with combined rates of 30 percent or more. If an Uber investor earns $100,000 from growth in the value of the stock, the investor would be subject only to capital gains taxes, at a rate of 15 percent.[22]

Some have argued that the tax code's preferential treatment of capital gains over income is justified because it encourages saving rather than spending. Savings benefit both the individual saver (by providing financial security) and society (by providing capital to support growth). But this justification doesn't explain why returns on investments that produce capital gains are taxed differently from returns produced by other savings vehicles. Many other forms of savings—savings accounts, certificates of deposit, Treasury bonds, and money market accounts, all of which are popular among many Americans, including those who might not invest in other ways—do not receive preferential treatment from the tax code, even though they provide financial security for the individual and capital for society.

This amounts to a double penalty: Americans who choose the security of these types of non-investment accounts receive a lower rate of return (granted, as one would expect of a lower-risk product) *and* pay a higher tax on those modest returns. Meanwhile, investors who have the financial resources to tolerate greater risk are doubly rewarded. The market is likely to deliver greater returns for riskier investments, and the tax system compounds those gains by taxing the earnings at a lower rate. It is not surprising that markets reward risky investments; it is unclear why the government does.

The discrepancy in returns from these different investments can be profound, even where risk is reduced by investing in a diversified portfolio. For example, a taxpayer who invested $100,000 in a compounding-growth savings account in 2013 might have $108,000 by the end of 2022; but a taxpayer who put the same $100,000 in an index fund at the same time would have more than $370,000 at the end of the same period.† With riskier investments, a similar experiment produces even greater earnings. A person who invested $100,000 in Apple when the company went public in 1980 would own stock worth more than $50 million dollars after forty years. Someone who invested $100,000 in Bitcoin in 2015 would have more than $20 million in the cryptocurrency nine years later.

---

† Savings account growth is calculated using the calculator at this website: https://historicalsavingscalculator.com. This was a time of unusually low interest rates, with annual returns many years at 1 percent or less. But even if rates were 5 percent throughout this period, the account would grow to only $163,000, and that is without taking into account annual taxes due on the interest income. The index fund returns are based on the S&P 500 and calculated at an annualized return of 12.4 percent (https://www.officialdata .org/us/stocks/s-p-500/2013?amount=100&endYear=2022).

Of course these examples are outliers. For every Apple or Bitcoin, there's another investment story where growth never happened or the investment went down in value, even to zero.[23] But individuals with resources can mitigate these risks by investing in a diverse portfolio. In addition, having some losses is not all bad, as they can be used strategically to offset gains on other more profitable investments when the assets are sold.

Many of the most profitable investment channels, including hedge funds, venture capital funds, and private equity investments, are available only to *accredited* investors. These are the wealthiest investors who meet the Securities and Exchange Commission's (SEC) definition of *accredited* by having earnings greater than $200,000 or assets, excluding their home, exceeding $1 million.[24] While these restrictions are ostensibly intended to protect investors with limited resources from risky ventures, they produce a major, additional tax-code advantage for wealthy people. Not only do these individuals have access to the most elite investment channels; they'll also pay less tax when those gains are realized.

But when and how do capital gains on an investment get *realized*? How does the tax code ensure the taxation of profits that are continually changing? The answer: Sometimes it doesn't.

The Deferral Gambit

The United States taxes money made on the sale of capital assets at a lower rate than money made as earnings from work. But the greater value of capital assets is in how the tax code treats them *before* they're sold, when they're still investments appreciating in value. Appreciating assets incur no tax at all—a phenomenon known as *deferral.*

As investments go up in value, investors owe no taxes on that gain until they sell the investment.[25] That sale is treated as a *realization* event. The rule, known as the *realization rule*, means that if an investor acquires stock for a small amount and then sees the stock grow to be worth millions (or, in the case of Bill Gates, Mark Zuckerberg, Elon Musk, Steve Ballmer, Sergey Brin, Warren Buffett, Larry Ellison, Larry Page, Michael Bloomberg, and others *billions*), no taxes are imposed on the gain unless it's sold. This lack of ongoing taxation allows for faster growth of wealth, especially for the wealthiest Americans, who can afford to leave investments untouched and unliquidated.

The massive growth of untaxed wealth in this century has prompted political leaders to propose new methods to impose taxes on wealth as it grows. These proposals have included wealth taxes (a low annual tax on total wealth) and mark-to-market taxes (annual capital gains taxes on net gains of property). In an attempt to undermine such initiatives, a group of wealthy Americans and antitax organizations funded a legal case that reached the Supreme Court in 2024, *Moore v. United States*, which aimed to impose a constitutional hurdle to taxing unrealized wealth. Their efforts were not entirely successful: The majority of the Court effectively sidestepped the issue while leaving it in play for a future case.[26]

Regardless of whether realization is constitutionally required for taxation, there are ample practical reasons to allow unrealized capital gains to go untaxed during an investor's life. Most importantly, gains that have not yet been realized, or secured by a sale, are ephemeral: They can come down in value just as easily as they can go up.[27] Many an investor has been flying high on the market value of stock only to later regret not having sold out when she could. That's the reason unrealized gains are known as *paper gains*: They're often fleeting.

The realization rule also avoids problems of valuation and liquidity. Mandatory annual taxation of gains would require the annual valuation of all investment properties. This is not a problem for investments with a readily available market—publicly traded stock or cryptocurrencies—but it would be considerably more complicated for everything else, such as closely held business interests, real estate, artwork, and other collectibles, which have no public indices of value. There's also a threat of unfairness to investors who don't have liquidity: without sale proceeds, taxpayers might not have the cash to pay the tax.

These reasons make it easy to understand why the realization rule was adopted, but its effect has been to provide enormous benefits to wealthy taxpayers by allowing them to control the timing of their capital gains and losses. This facilitates endless opportunities for tax avoidance, prompting many tax scholars to describe the realization rule as the Achilles' heel of the tax system.[28] As the tax scholar Marjorie Kornhauser has described it: "Realization causes economic distortion, creates inequity among some taxpayers generates much of the complexity of the tax law, and provides may opportunities for taxpayers to manipulate their tax status to achieve desired consequences."[29]

The deferral of taxes on capital assets is so valuable for investors because it allows for uninterrupted, compounding growth of wealth over time, undiminished by taxes. Experts have compared this situation to receiving an interest-free loan from the government that can then be invested to produce more income.[30] The longer the deferral, the greater the benefit.[31] Add to deferral the preferential tax rates for capital gains, and the accumulating effect of the advantages is staggering.

To understand how great the value of deferral can be, consider two people, each of whom is able to set aside $100,000 for twenty years for the same rate of return. One puts the money in a bank account and reinvests the interest each year; the other purchases stock. Both investments grow at a rate of 10 percent a year, one through interest and the other through the growth in value of the stock. The only difference is that the income from the bank account is subject to annual income taxes (at a rate as high as 37 percent), whereas the stock is subject to no taxes until it is sold and the gains are realized. Because of this difference in tax treatment, at the end of twenty years, the bank account will be worth $340,000; the stock will be worth $647,000. Even after the sale of the stock, and imposition of maximum capital gains taxes of 20 percent on the gain, the stock investment would still be worth over $537,000, producing almost $200,000 more than the deposit in the bank account with identical rates of return.[32]

Beyond the financial advantages of deferral, the realization rule also enables property owners to time their sales for maximum tax advantage. This is most commonly done by cherry-picking the sale of different assets in order to offset realized capital gains with capital losses. This *tax-loss harvesting* is particularly easy for wealthy investors with diverse portfolios, where there is a good likelihood that at any one time some investments will have produced losses.

The Angel of Death Loophole

As we have seen, there are plenty of good reasons to allow deferral of gains so long as a person continues to own an asset. But that doesn't mean the asset should avoid taxes altogether. Both President Nixon and President Obama proposed rules that would impose capital gains taxes on gains when property is transferred by gift or at death, just the same as if the property had been sold. This rule, called *deemed realization*, has been in place in Canada since 1972.[33]

By contrast, the United States does *not* tax gains on property given away during life or transferred at death. And in the greatest giveaway of all, for transfers occurring at death, the tax code actually washes away all gains accrued to the asset during the life of the deceased. The property received by the heirs is treated as if they had bought it at fair market value. This, in turn, allows them to sell it tax-free. In technical terms, this provision is called a *step up in basis*; in more casual terms, it's known as the *Angel of Death loophole*. The effect of the loophole is that capital gains held until death are never subject to tax. If someone purchased $1 million worth of NASDAQ-listed stocks in 2004, the value of those stocks would have grown to $22 million in 2024. That investor would pay no taxes during his life, and when he died, his heirs would be treated as if they'd bought the stock themselves for $22 million; the $21 million gain would not exist, as least in terms of taxes. This loophole can be used again and again within families, allowing for ever-greater growth and concentrations of wealth as property passes from generation to generation.‡

The ability of people to avoid all capital gains at their death has a larger, distortionary effect on the market. In the economy, people count on market prices to reflect actual value. But the allure of paying zero tax on an appreciated asset incentivizes people to hold on to an asset they might otherwise sell, a dynamic known as the *lock-in effect*. Rather perversely, some people have cited the lock-in effect as reason to further reduce capital gains rates, as a way to induce people to sell before death. Of course, there is no tax rate that will ever beat zero tax. A fairer and

‡ Property passed by gift does not provide the same total washing away of gains as occurs when property is passed at death or donated to charity. However, that doesn't mean that the gains will ever be subject to tax, because the transfer of appreciated property by gift is still tax-free for the donor. This leaves the recipient with the same opportunities to avoid taxes that the donor had. If the recipient sells the property, they will pay capital gains taxes, but if they simply borrow against it, and then pass it on at death or donate it to charity, all gains will still be wiped out.

more efficient way to address the problem of the lock-in effect would be to close the loophole that gave rise to it in the first place, by adopting the rule that unrealized gains should be taxed when property is transferred by gift or at death, just the same as when transferred by sale.

Stock Buybacks

Despite two major financial crises already this century, the stock market during this period has proved a surprisingly reliable tool for individuals seeking to grow capital outside the purview of the tax code (at least for those who can afford to invest for longer time horizons). This reflects a marked difference from the period 1915–1982.

Prior to 1982, the only way companies could legally share profits with their investors was by issuing dividends—cash payouts to investors based on the company's profits. The dominance of dividends at that time is reflected in the fact that dividends provided 73 percent of all returns from stock investments in the 1970s.[34]

One reason for the popularity of dividends was that they provided the safest option for those who wanted to profit from investing in the stock market: Pre-1982 investors who counted on the growing value of their stock rather than dividend income were less likely to be rewarded by the market. A look at the history of the Dow Jones Industrial Average illustrates why this is the case. From 1915 to 1982, the Dow, adjusted for inflation, largely fluctuated between 2,000 and 7,000, but with no observable pattern, and it

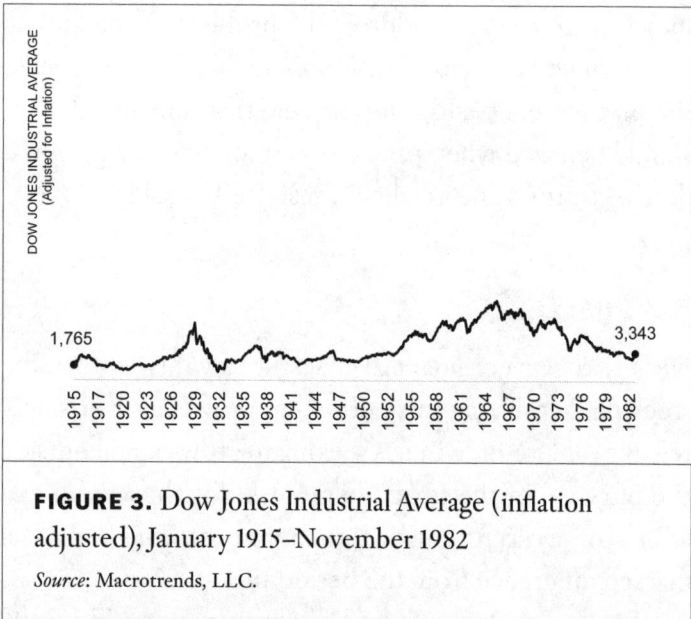

FIGURE 3. Dow Jones Industrial Average (inflation adjusted), January 1915–November 1982

Source: Macrotrends, LLC.

never passed 10,000. The lack of regular growth in the market more broadly is also reflected in the fact that the Dow hovered around 3,000 at different points in the twentieth century: 1927, 1935, 1945, 1952, and 1982.[35] Given this uncertainty around benefits of the stock market's capital growth, it's little wonder that investors chose companies that distributed profits through dividends; the stock market wasn't reliable for much else.

In terms of taxing profits from investments, investors' preference for dividends benefited the federal government: Between 1954 and 2003, dividends were subject to the same high tax rate as workers' earnings. The reliance on dividends for returns on investments, combined with the high tax rate on those dividends, meant that wealthy Americans were generally subject to high taxes on their investment returns.

A pronounced shift in the market occurred after 1982, when an obscure SEC rule created a new way for companies to distribute profits to their shareholders: buying back their own stock on the open market. When companies buy their own stock, it increases the sale price of the stock by adding buyers to the market (the company itself) and by reducing the total number of shares. The shift to stock buybacks from dividends also has reduced the tax liability of rich investors by moving them from recipients of taxable dividends to holders of stock that enjoys tax-free growth in value.

The rule change was dramatic: Prior to 1982, the SEC had considered companies that purchased their own stock to be engaged in a form of illegal market manipulation—so much so that when the SEC moved to allow stock buybacks, it still warned in a public comment that buybacks threatened to disrupt investors' and shareholders' ability "to rely on a market that is set by independent market forces and not influenced in any manipulative manner by the issuer or persons closely related to the issuer."[36] The SEC still made the change, for the first time allowing companies to manipulate the market price of their stock by using their profits to buy back their own shares on the open market.

After this rule change, many publicly traded companies switched to buying back stock and stopped issuing dividends. From 1990 to 2020, less than 17 percent of investors' returns came from dividends (as compared to 73 percent in the 1970s). This phenomenon is known as the *disappearing dividends.*[37]

Stock buybacks benefit senior management as well, who largely are often compensated on the basis of increases in stock value.[38] This has especially been the case since the early 1990s, when companies began compensating senior executives with company stock options.[39] For example, in 2024, CEOs of large, publicly traded companies received, on average, 70 percent of their compensation in stock.[40]

Since the time of this rule change allowing stock buybacks, stocks have skyrocketed in value. The value of the Dow Jones in 1982 was $3,000; it climbed steadily over the next forty-three years to be worth more than $43,000.

Shifting from dividends to stock buybacks effectively transformed one type of return (dividend income, which was taxed at high rates) to capital appreciation (eligible for deferral, thereby perhaps never taxed at all). Even though in 2003 Congress reduced the tax rate on dividends to 15 percent, it's hard to beat a rate of zero, which remains available first through deferral and then through the Angel of Death loophole.

Investment in capital assets, deferral, and the Angel of Death loophole together are the core of "buy, borrow, die" as a tax-planning technique.[41] This series of mechanisms starts with buying a capital asset (like stock or other investments), and when it goes up in value, rather than selling it

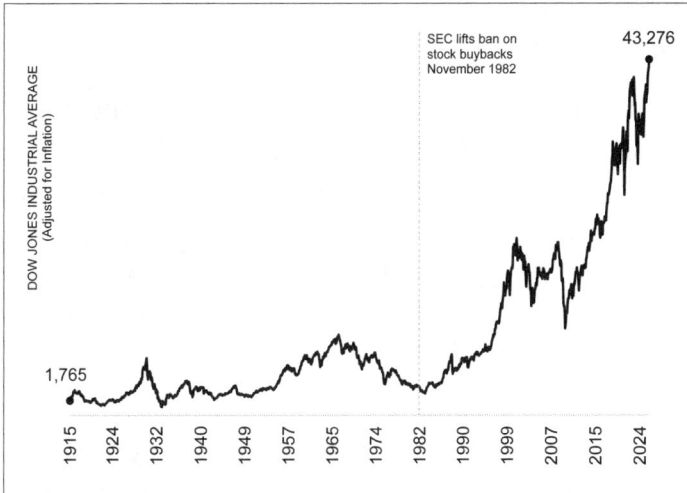

FIGURE 4. Dow Jones Industrial Average (inflation adjusted), January 1915–October 2024

Source: Macrotrends, LLC.

(which would generate a tax liability), it is used as collateral for a loan, which allows the investor to access cash. No taxes are due on the loan proceeds, because the property has still not been sold, and interest payments on the loan are often tax deductible as well. Loan proceeds can be used to buy houses, yachts, and other things that support the asset owner's lifestyle. When a loan comes due, it can be repaid either with a new loan or, if the asset's owner has died, from the tax-free sale of property after death. Buy, borrow, die is one reason Americans who are wealthy enough to be able to live off their investments are also lucky enough to avoid income taxes altogether on their profits.

Borrowing by Those with Plenty

Borrowing against assets is an extraordinarily popular way for rich Americans to finance their lifestyles while avoiding income taxes. As one wealth adviser describes the advantages of borrowing: "You could buy a boat, you could go to Disney World, you could buy a company. . . . The tax benefits are stunning."[42] These benefits are particularly valuable for the richest Americans, who have plenty of willing creditors and—since they would otherwise be subject to tax at the highest rates—the most to gain by not paying taxes.

Larry Ellison, the founder of Oracle Corporation, is one of the richest people in the world, with wealth in 2024 in excess of $230 billion. Ellison has long practiced the art of borrowing to support his lifestyle. As far back as 2002, Ellison had borrowed and spent so much money on homes and high-end assets, including a $194 million yacht, that his accountant famously advised him to "slow down" with his spending because "his spending was like a 'freight train' hitting a 'debt wall.'"[43]

Since then, Ellison has continued his practice of debt-financed spending, including the purchase of most of Hawaii's sixth-largest island, Lanai. That purchase has enabled Ellison to simultaneously create a playground for the rich and a modern-day company town: Ellison now owns virtually all the businesses on the island, including two Four Seasons resorts, the only non–Four Seasons hotel, the island's main grocery store, the only gas station, and the community newspaper. In effect, Ellison is now the boss, landlord, or both to the island's three thousand inhabitants—a stunning experiment in opulence and power. According to one article, many residents both rent from him and work for him and a provision in his residential leases say that if you're terminated from a job with any of his companies, you can be kicked out of your home too.[44] Residents say that no other entity can balance Ellison's control, so his decisions carry the weight of law, with minimal discussions of new projects and almost no due process.[45] Ellison has been able to make these and other purchases using untaxed dollars while still retaining his controlling ownership interest in Oracle by pledging over $30 billion worth of his Oracle stock as collateral for private loans.

Ellison is not alone. A 2021 *Forbes* analysis concluded that about 20 percent of *Forbes*'s four hundred billionaires whose primary wealth was in publicly traded firms had pledged substantial amounts of stock to secure borrowing. As of November 2021, that group had pledged stock worth over $185 billion.[46] Pledging—using stock as collateral to secure loans—poses financial risks that extend beyond the borrower. It also leaves other company investors open to the risk of margin calls: demands by the lender for more cash or assets to make up for a loss in share value. Margin calls can result in the forced sale of shares, devastating a company's share value.[47] For example, Green Mountain Coffee's founder Robert Stiller used significant portions of his shares in the company to fund a luxurious lifestyle, but when his borrowing habits were revealed in 2012, he was forced to sell $126 million of his shares in a single day to cover margin calls, spooking investors and driving Green Mountain Coffee to remove him as board chair.[48] Similarly, in May 2023, a speculator released a report on billionaire Carl Icahn's investment company, Icahn Enterprises (IEP), showing that Icahn had pledged over 50 percent of the total shares in the company. In response, IEP's value dropped by roughly 40 percent in a matter of days, and Icahn was forced to renegotiate his personal loans to untie them from IEP stock.[49] More broadly than these examples, significant corporate pledging creates what the corporate governance adviser Jun Frank calls "a mismatch between the control you can exercise over the company and the economic interest you have in the company."[50]

Because of these concerns, more than two-thirds of S&P 500 companies ban company employees and shareholders from pledging shares as collateral; only 3.4 percent fully permit the practice. However, over 20 percent of the companies that broadly prohibit pledging still grant exemptions to it, typically to their most powerful shareholders.[51] Most notably, Oracle bans all directors and executive officers from pledging company shares, with the single exception of one individual: Larry Ellison. Oracle is not alone in bowing to the interests of its largest shareholder. The publicly traded medical conglomerate Danaher Corporation exempted its cofounders, brothers Mitchell and Steven Rales, from its ban on pledging, stating simply, "[Their] shares had been pledged for decades." The two founders have pledged over 85 percent of their respective shares, leaving Danaher vulnerable to a potential margin call.[52]

Some companies are more discreet when making special deals for insiders. For example, the oil and gas pipeline firm Kinder Morgan prohibits the pledging of shares based on the individual's annual salary.[53] These rules require corporate insiders to retain full ownership of shares equal to three times their salary, meaning if they make $1 million a year, they can pledge only shares that they own in excess of $3 million. While such a system imposes meaningful limitations on many employees, that is not the case for the founder and executive chairman Richard Kinder, who (no surprise) is paid an annual salary of $1 but retains shares in the company. This not only allows him to avoid high taxes on earnings but also effectively allows him to pledge as many shares as he'd like, a perk he's taken full advantage of, at one time having pledged $679 million worth of Kinder Morgan shares.[54]

Who benefits from the system in which wealth from investment growth is subject to little or no taxes? By any measure, the wealthiest Americans do, as they have the most investments. In the twenty-first century, as wealth has become more concentrated in fewer hands, the benefits of that wealth have also become more concentrated. Lower capital gains tax rates have also disproportionately benefited those with high incomes. In 2022, more than 70 percent of the tax benefit went to those taxpayers with incomes over $1 million.[55] Many Americans investing in the stock market through their retirement plans might think that they too benefit from the capital gains rules; this is not the case. Retirement plans are subject to their own rules, and regardless of how the funds are invested, retirees who take distributions from these accounts must pay ordinary income tax rates on the full value of those distributions.[§]

STRATEGY 3: INHERIT WEALTH— EVEN BETTER THAN IT SOUNDS

The American tax code imposes its greatest burdens on those who work for their income and fewer burdens on those who make money from investments. But the absolute best way, bar none, to make wealth and avoid taxes is to do it the old-fashioned way: by inheriting it.[56]

Indeed, for all the public focus on high-profile wealthy individuals like Musk, Bezos, Buffett, and Gates, all of whom built their wealth by starting businesses, 121 of the 400 richest people according to *Forbes* in 2023 were simply fortunate inheritors.[57] Inheriting wealth is how Jacqueline, John, and Forrest Jr., and Marijke, Pamela, Valerie, and Victoria Mars, acquired their combined $116 billion as third- and fourth-generation heirs of Franklin Mars, who founded the Mars candy company in the early 1900s. It's how Nancy, Ann, Christy, Lukas, Alice, Rob, and Jim Walton acquired their combined $256 billion as heirs to Sam and Bud Walton, who founded Walmart in the 1960s.

Individuals who inherit wealth are fortunate in another way: Unlike those who receive almost any other type of

§ These are the rules for regular retirement accounts. Roth accounts are subject to different rules.

income, people who receive gifts, inheritances, life insurance payouts, or many types of distributions from trusts typically do so entirely free from income tax. In the US, inheritance, in its many forms, is excluded from the definition of *income*.[58] So, if an individual earns $1 million, she will pay about $375,000 in income and payroll taxes; if she receives $1 million as a gift, bequest, or proceeds from a life insurance policy, she will receive it entirely tax-free. Importantly, this exclusion from income taxes applies regardless of whether any estate or gift taxes are paid on the transfer.

Gifts and inheritances were originally treated as income, but they were removed—with no discussion—from the 1913 version of the tax code.[59] The tax scholar Richard Schmalbeck suggests that the decision to exclude gifts and inheritances was "simply a tale of the triumph of lobbyists."[60] As a result of the exclusion, a person can inherit $10 million or $100 billion and owe no income taxes on the receipt of that property.

Life insurance is a surprising part of the gift and inheritance privilege. Not only are life insurance payouts untaxed; certain life insurance policies also provide other tax-avoidance benefits. The benefits of life insurance have been justified by the industry because of the role life insurance plays in protecting surviving family members when a chief breadwinner dies. This narrative is increasingly detached from the realities of who benefits from life insurance policies, however. Increasingly, the business of life insurance is not to serve vulnerable families but to serve the wealthy, by providing a vehicle for tax-free growth and the transfer of intergenerational wealth.[61] These benefits are seen in *private placement life insurance*—a vehicle available only to accredited investors—that allows the wealthiest Americans to use their life insurance policies to invest in hedge funds and other high-risk investments. As of 2024, an estimated $40 billion or more was set aside in such accounts in the US, all of which will pass tax-free to wealthy heirs.[62]

The tax system benefits these wealthy heirs in another way as well: by hiding these tax benefits from the public. Gifts and inheritances are not only received free of income tax; but their receipt is also free of reporting requirements.** This lack of reporting helps perpetuate the myth that the tax liability of the wealthy is more burdensome than it is.

To illustrate: a person with a $1 million salary (subject to about $325,000 in income taxes) also receives a $10 million inheritance. Under current reporting rules, only the $1 million salary is reported on the taxpayer's return, giving the impression—to the taxpayer, the IRS, and the public— that the taxpayer is paying income taxes at a rate of 32.5 percent. On the other hand, if the taxpayer were required to *report* the $10 million inheritance (even if it weren't subject to tax!), it would be easier to see that the actual tax burden is less than 4 percent of the income acquired in that year.

** Although some gifts and inheritances are reported to the government under the estate and gift tax code, because of the generous exemptions, as well as loopholes and valuation-gaming opportunities, this captures just a small amount of the funds eventually received by heirs.

If we add more zeros to the inheritance, the tax liability shrinks even more.

There are many other examples of the tax system requiring taxpayers to report income even when that income is not subject to tax. Income from tax-exempt bonds, distributions from Roth IRAs, and capital gains on the sale of a house must all be reported on taxpayers' annual tax returns even though they are not subject to tax. This reporting plays a valuable function because it helps policymakers determine the cost to the federal government of excluding these items from taxation. (These tax benefits are officially called *tax expenditures*—to reflect the fact that they have the same impact on the budget as direct spending—and are reported annually on a tax expenditure budget.[63]) Failure to require such reporting for gifts and inheritances keeps us all in the dark and opens the door to plausible misinformation on the tax burden of the wealthy.

By following the tenets of the Tax-Avoidance Playbook, the wealthy avoid the tax burdens that normally apply to earnings while also avoiding income taxes on investments and inheritances. That leaves only one plank of the tax code—estate and gift taxes—to do the work of subjecting wealth to tax where income and capital gains taxes fail. By definition, estate and gift taxes apply broadly to all property transferred during life and at death, seemingly providing adequate backup to the inadequacies of the income tax system. However, since 1990, these taxes have been quietly dismantled, to the point that they are little more than paper tigers—giving moral cover to the wealthy while imposing little cost on them. The evidence is in the numbers: Although the wealth of the richest 1 percent was over $46 trillion in 2024, the estate and gift tax generated only $30 billion in taxes, about 0.05 percent of total federal revenue. In sharp contrast, 36 percent of federal revenue is raised from payroll taxes and 49 percent from income taxes.

The next chapter explains how this has been allowed to happen.

3 JUBILEE

Dan Duncan was born in rural Shelby County, Texas, in 1933. He gained modest fame during the twentieth century as a Texas oil tycoon, philanthropist, and avid big-game hunter. But his greatest notoriety occurred only in death: In 2010, Duncan became the first billionaire in American history to pass the entirety of his wealth—an estimated $9 billion—to his heirs without paying a penny of federal taxes in doing so.[1]

The Duncan heirs paid no tax on receipt of the property because, unlike almost all other types of income, including found money and lottery winnings, recipients of inheritances are not subject to income taxes on property they inherit. Had he died one year earlier or later, the transfer of wealth would have been subject to estate taxes at rates of either 35 percent or 45 percent.[2] This was not the case when Duncan died in 2010, which was the one-year "tax jubilee" that President George W. Bush had put in place nine years earlier—part of his failed drive to repeal the tax entirely.[3]

Although Duncan was the first, he was not the only billionaire to benefit from the one-year tax holiday. Before the end of 2010, five billionaires (along with thousands of multimillionaires) had passed billions of dollars tax-free to their heirs, at a cost to American taxpayers of more than $45 billion in forgone federal revenue.[4]

Taxes on inherited wealth have played an important role throughout American history and economy, both in funding the government and in curtailing large accumulations of inherited wealth. Such financial consolidation has historically been viewed as a threat to democracy and antithetical to the country's founding principles. Yet today—with wealth accumulating at levels not seen since the Gilded Age and with growing concerns about the impact of plutocratic wealth on American democracy—the estate tax is in a moribund state. Its easy avoidance has made it a shell of its former self, and paths to avoiding it are readily available to anyone with a tax adviser.[5]

THE ANTI-INHERITANCE STATE

The founders of the United States sought to create a country based on republican principles of equality. One problem they faced in doing so was managing inherited wealth.[6] The new nation had been founded in direct opposition to the entrenched aristocracies of England and continental

Europe, where wealth and power devolved through family inheritance.[7] Avoiding this fate in the United States was a matter of critical concern, particularly for Thomas Jefferson, who wrote to John Adams about the need for the nation to distinguish between the "natural aristocracy based on virtue and talents" and the threat of the "artificial aristocracy" based on wealth and birth. As Jefferson wrote, "The artificial aristocracy is a mischievous ingredient in government, and provision should be made to prevent its ascendancy."[8]

Jefferson's most immediate tool for limiting the impact of inherited wealth was to change the English rules of inheritance that had been in force in the US during the colonial period.[9] England had long preserved family wealth and privilege through the system known as primogeniture, in which land passed to the eldest male son (or in the absence of a son, to the eldest male heir).[10] Primogeniture has provided endless plot points for English stories—from *Pride and Prejudice* to *Downton Abbey*—on the problems faced by families with daughters instead of sons. The system also maximized the power of dynastic wealth by keeping property together and under the control of a single heir across generations.

By contrast, the US rejection of primogeniture meant that large accumulations of inherited wealth were less likely to occur, because family property was divided among multiple children rather than consolidated under just one. In 1830, Alexis de Tocqueville noted this lack of hereditary wealth and saw it as playing a central role in shaping the

American work ethic: "Amongst a democratic people, where there is no hereditary wealth, every man works to earn a living, or has worked, or is born of parents who have worked. The notion of labor is therefore presented to the mind on every side as the necessary, natural, and honest condition of human existence."[11]

In addition to altering inheritance rules to encourage the breakup of inherited wealth, the new nation was quick to tax inherited wealth when the country faced financial needs. Whenever there was a need for additional revenue—to fund the creation of the country's first navy, to finance the Civil War, to finance the Spanish-American War—the first place the country turned was taxes on inherited wealth.

This system worked well enough to keep inherited wealth in check during the country's first century, but the post–Civil War industrialization period produced a seismic shift. Mark Twain satirically referred to this time in the late nineteenth century as the Gilded Age, reflecting his belief that American elites had gilded over the deep-seated social and economic divides.[12] During the period, figures like Cornelius Vanderbilt, John D. Rockefeller, Andrew Carnegie, J. P. Morgan, Andrew Mellon, and other "robber barons" amassed enormous fortunes by securing monopolistic control over steel, petroleum, railroads, tobacco, and other industries that had undergone explosive growth in that era due to the development of new technologies.[13] Faced with no meaningful taxes or government regulation, these men's riches grew at exponential rates and were passed on, relatively undiminished, to the next generation.[14]

This growth in wealth brought about transformational changes in society. As the historian Steve Fraser describes, by the end of the nineteenth century, American society, "which had prided itself on being a nation of small producers, skilled workers, farmers, all roughly equal in their social position, was no longer that." Instead, America "was overwhelmingly a nation of very powerful concentrated wealth on the one hand, and wage labor on the other suffering a very serious dilemma about how they would survive."[15] This extreme inequality was captured in the 1890s by the rising Populist Party, whose platform characterized the rapid industrialization of the country as having led to the development of two great classes: "tramps and millionaires."[16]

The power of the industrialists (and their heirs) was felt across all levels of society. "The workers, farmers, small businessmen, and professional men suffered frustration in their attempts to lead a rich and independent life in a society which professed democracy, but which in actuality was dominated politically and economically by an oligarchy, [the captains of industry and finance, and their political henchman]," wrote the tax historian Sidney Ratner.[17]

These harms were documented by investigative journalists and writers of the time who revealed corrupt and abusive practices by the country's titans of industry. These included Ida Tarbell's exposé in *McClure's Magazine* on Rockefeller's Standard Oil, including its practice of rigging railroad prices to smother competition, and Upton Sinclair's depiction in *The Jungle* of the perils of unsafe working conditions and unsanitary practices in the Chicago meatpacking industry.

This new reality—powerful oligarchs throwing around their weight to the detriment of the common man—was seen as a threat to democracy. As an opinion piece in the *New York Post* warned readers in 1900: "Every republic runs its greatest risk not from discontented soldiers, as from discontented multi-millionaires." All previous republics, the writer noted, had been "overthrown by rich men." This could happen in America, too, as monopoly capitalists were "deriding the Constitution, unrebuked by the executive or by public opinion."[18]

As the industrialists passed wealth to their heirs, they created a new class of idle American rich, many of whom embraced aristocratic ways. In its short history, the US had sought to define itself in contrast to the aristocracies of England and Europe, so much so that the founders adopted provisions in the Constitution specifically prohibiting titles of nobility.[19] And yet, less than a century later, the most powerful Americans were adopting the trappings of the noble class: living in palaces, commissioning coats of arms, dressing their servants in livery, and even wearing crowns. The desire for aristocratic status was so great that wealthy American families married off hundreds of daughters into European aristocratic families—sometimes against their will—to enable them to achieve the titles of nobility and family status that the American Constitution frustratingly disallowed.[20]

None of this was secret, or even discreet. Indeed, it was quite the opposite. In his 1899 *The Theory of the Leisure Class*, the economist Thorstein Veblen coined the term *conspicuous consumption* to describe the means by which the country's "leisure class" attained elevated social status, including performative expressions of wealth.[21] Their ostentatious consumption often took place in the form of lavish parties, including some that featured such excesses as live elephants serving champagne and cigars wrapped in hundred-dollar bills distributed as party favors—all of it well publicized to the press.[22]

Conspicuous consumption by the superrich was particularly jarring when set in contrast to the lives of the urban poor, documented by the photographer Jacob Riis in his book *How the Other Half Lives* (1890). Riis's work, set against the public awareness of the opulent lifestyles enjoyed by America's wealthy class, produced a familiar public tension over the uneven distributions of capitalism—and with it, concern among some that Americans would embrace socialism, whose principles had increasing appeal among workers, farmers, and the middle class in the waning nineteenth century.[23]

Economists and public intellectuals in the 1880s debated how the country should address its nascent American aristocracy, whose extraordinary social and political power had been acquired by inheritance rather than by merit. For many, the answer was to impose limitations on inherited wealth.[24] One of these was Charles Bellamy. In his 1884 book *The Way Out*, Bellamy called for the government to impose a cap on the amount any person could distribute by will as a way of addressing the growing American aristocracy of wealth. Bellamy was particularly concerned about how the wealthy rejected America's principles of equality among classes and "spurn with their feet the classes that work," adding that the American aristocracy—"as complete and insufferable an aristocracy as the most antiquated nation of Europe"—had outdone their predecessors from across the Atlantic in creating "an aristocracy of wealth."[25]

Other writers highlighted the connection between inheritance taxes and the founders' concerns about the pernicious effect of inherited wealth on democracy. In the widely read 1886 book *Taxation in American States and Cities*, the economist Richard T. Ely reminded readers that the founders rejected hereditary privileges with the aim of forcing "each one to rely on his own exertions for his own fortunes, desiring to give to all as nearly as practicable an equal start in the race of life." Ely suggested that a graduated inheritance tax "would be in accord with the principles of Jeffersonian democracy and some of the best modern thinkers on economic and social topics."[26]

Ely also warned that far more radical measures were being proposed by "conservative men," including an 1886 committee of the Illinois Bar Association that supported imposing an overall cap on inherited wealth. The report admonished that "there never was a time in the history of the world when the power of money in skillful hands was so great as the present." Ely characterized the American fin de siècle as a moment requiring reform: The country had grown into a worse version of the thing it had rejected a century earlier.[27]

The case for imposing heavy taxes on inherited wealth received a tremendous boost from a surprising source: Andrew Carnegie, one of America's richest men. Carnegie's life was a rags-to-riches story, not uncommon among the first industrialists. A poor immigrant from Scotland, Carnegie began working at age thirteen in a cotton mill, then as a telegraph operator at the Pennsylvania Railroad. Through investments and shrewd business alignments, as well as ruthless union busting, Carnegie eventually earned his fortune through his ownership of Carnegie Steel Company, later US Steel, the most profitable industrial enterprise in the world. When Carnegie sold his company to J. P. Morgan in 1901 for $303 million (about $10 billion in 2024 dollars), he possessed the greatest fortune ever amassed by an American.

After retiring, Carnegie devoted the last fifteen years of his life to large-scale philanthropy, including funding more than three thousand libraries. He also became a prolific writer and public commentator. From 1882 to 1916, Carnegie published eight books, sixty-three articles, and ten public addresses in pamphlet form. Carnegie's writings were published in all the leading journals of his day, and his down-to-earth writing style made him popular with people of all ages and backgrounds.

Carnegie's most famous essay, "The Gospel of Wealth," published in June 1890, addressed what he considered the most pressing issue of his time: how to handle the social divisions caused by extreme concentrations of wealth, or as Carnegie described it, "the proper administration of wealth, so that the ties of brotherhood may still bind together the rich and poor in harmonious relationship."[28]

According to Carnegie, not all wealth inequality was a problem, because the creation of wealth ultimately served to the betterment of the masses, "such that the least wealthy people lived better than the wealthiest of their forebears."[29] He also made clear that his concern was not with "moderate sums saved by many years of effort, the returns on which are required for the comfortable maintenance and education of families."[30] The focus of Carnegie's concern was whether the wealthy should be able to pass "great fortunes" down to the next generation. Here, Carnegie was an adamant no: "Why should men leave great fortunes to their children? If this is done from affection, is it not misguided affection? Observation teaches that, generally speaking, it is not well for the children that they should be so burdened. Neither is it well for the state. . . . Wise men will soon conclude that, for the best interests of the members of their families and of the state, such bequests are an improper use of their means."[31]

Carnegie argued that the best thing for wealthy people to do was to give their money away to good causes during their lifetimes. But for those who chose not to, Carnegie strongly supported heavy estate taxes: "Of all forms of taxation, [the estate tax] seems the wisest. Men who continue hoarding great sums all their lives, the proper use of which for public ends would work good to the community, should be made to feel that the community, in the form of the state, cannot thus be deprived of its proper share. By taxing estates heavily at death, the state marks its condemnation of the selfish millionaire's unworthy life."[32]

The essay had a significant impact on the development of political support for the imposing of heavy estate taxes. As a result, taxes were not just supported by the radical left but also by moderate progressives and even some conservatives.[33]

Of course, some of this support may have been rooted as much in fear as in aspiration. In 1895, Frederick Judson, later president of the American Political Science Association, warned that "injustice in taxation aroused the most dangerous class spirit," adding that "capitalists should establish justice and equality in taxation in order to enjoy security of property."[34] Even the conservative *Wall Street Journal* ran an article calling for an inheritance tax, arguing that the "involuntary rich" needed to be saved from themselves so as not to fall into a life of "idleness and profligacy," the moral effect of which would be "disastrous" to poor and rich alike: "These conditions," the paper argued, "raise an inheritance tax to the level of a national blessing."[35]

As America debated its inherited-wealth problem during the final quarter of the nineteenth century, it was England that took the first step in imposing a tax through its Finance Bill of 1894.[36] Soon other countries followed, and the United States found itself playing catch-up with the more egalitarian systems from which it had previously sought to disassociate.

TARIFFS TURN TO TAXING THE RICH, 1900–1990

Public discussions at the turn of the century focused on the importance of imposing high inheritance taxes on the wealthy, but the reality on the ground was very different. Throughout the nineteenth century and into the twentieth century, federal revenue came almost exclusively from taxes on imports—tariffs. From the earliest days of the republic, American politicians, backed by business interests who sought to avoid competition and keep prices high, argued that tariffs were vital to the creation of vibrant domestic industry.[37] The most prominent of these advocates was William McKinley, who ran in his 1896 presidential campaign as "a Tariff man, standing on a Tariff platform." In doing so, he raised an unprecedented $3.5 million in campaign contributions from corporate and banking interests, largely by convincing American industrialists that the Democratic nominee, the populist Williams Jennings Bryan, planned to slash tariffs. For his part Bryan argued that the system of protective tariffs was "held together by the cohesive power of plunder," benefiting the interests of the protected at the expense of most working people and consumers. With this approach, Bryan raised only one-fifth as much in campaign contributions as McKinley did, and Bryan was defeated.[38]

President McKinley followed through with his protectionist plans, raising tariffs to new heights through the Dingley Tariff, which raised these taxes by an average of 57 percent and raised the cost of living by nearly 25 percent. This system was not without its critics: Many noted that the prohibitively high tariffs benefited industrialists (who were saved from competition from foreign providers) at the expense of farmers and other consumers, who had to purchase foreign goods at inflated prices or deal with domestic producers who didn't have to compete with the international markets on quality or price.[39]

The election of 1900 reconvened the 1896 election, with McKinley and Bryan again squaring off for the presidency. However, this time, McKinley's running mate was a very unlikely partner: the progressive Theodore Roosevelt. As governor of New York, Roosevelt had alienated Republican Party bosses by pushing a tax on corporate franchises. Anxious to be rid of the meddlesome young governor, and hoping he could provide some populist credentials to McKinley's campaign, the party bosses kicked him upstairs into the vice presidency, where they hoped he could cause less trouble.

In 1901, an assassin's bullet ended McKinley's presidency and began Roosevelt's—a position from which the latter immediately moved to promote his progressive and populist ideas across the country, including heavy taxation on the inheritances of the rich. As the scion of a wealthy New York society family, Roosevelt might have seemed an unlikely proponent of heavy taxes on the rich. But his personal experience (including as someone who overcame great hardships, having been a sickly, asthmatic child) fed his contempt for the leisure class. Roosevelt expressed his feelings for members of the New York society set in an 1895 essay. "There is not in the world a more ignoble character than the mere money-getting American, insensible to every duty, regardless of every principle, bent only on amassing a fortune, and putting his fortune to only the basest uses," he wrote. "They are curses to the country."[40]

Roosevelt's portrayal of New York's high society rings today as politically radical, but his messaging was motivated by more practical concerns as well. Roosevelt was strongly motivated to preserve America's capitalist system against the risks of socialism. The best way of doing so, it seemed, was to raise the standard of living for the masses and work to prevent gross abuses of power by the privileged class.[41]

The president's fears about threats to capitalism were not just theoretical: American anarchists and socialists were growing in prominence. Following McKinley's assassination, his killer, the anarchist Leon Czolgosz, said before his execution: "I killed the President because he was the enemy of the good people—the good working people."[42]

Eliminating capitalism was a key platform item of the Socialist Party, which by the early twentieth century had attracted the support of a broad swath of the public dissatisfied with what unfettered capitalism had wrought. Immigrant and native-born workers and their families, tenant farmers, middle-class intellectuals, socially conscious millionaires, urban reformers, and feminists all joined the movement.[43] Eugene V. Debs, the Socialist candidate, twice won over nine hundred thousand votes, in the 1912 and 1920 presidential elections, while the party also elected two US representatives, dozens of state legislators, more than one hundred mayors, and countless other officials.[44] In addition, more than three hundred English and foreign-language socialist periodicals were in circulation, some with numbers of subscribers that rivaled the major urban daily newspapers.[45]

To quell the threats behind these developments, in his annual message to Congress in 1906, Roosevelt called for "the adoption of some such scheme as that of a progressive tax on all fortunes, beyond a certain amount, either given in life or devised or bequeathed upon death to any individual."[46] Roosevelt was particularly interested in placing "a constantly increasing burden on the inheritance of those swollen fortunes which it is certainly of no benefit to this country to perpetuate."[47] While attempts to pass the estate tax failed during the early years of the first decade of the twentieth century, war in Europe changed that.

As World War I disrupted American trade relationships, revenues from tariffs were drastically reduced.[48] To make up for the lost revenue and to raise additional funds to finance the impending entrance into the war by the US, Congress turned to taxing the rich. The first step was to pass a constitutional amendment allowing for the adoption of an income tax system (which the Supreme Court had found unconstitutional in 1895).[49] The Sixteenth Amendment was ratified in 1913, and a new income tax was adopted later that year. At first, this income tax imposed taxes at very modest rates (the highest rate was 7 percent), but in 1917, it was amended to impose significantly higher rates on top earners (as high as 73 percent).[50] A progressive estate tax was passed in 1916.[51] These taxes—along with a wartime tax on excess business profits—kicked off a sea change in federal taxation: Tax burdens were shifted away from those with little means to those with higher incomes and substantial wealth, with taxes assessed in accordance with their ability to pay.[52] While concerns with wealth inequality laid the groundwork for this shift toward taxing the rich, the change might not have occurred but for the country's entrance into World War I.

The political scientists Kenneth Scheve and David Stasavage studied twenty countries, exploring the question of when, over the course of their histories, the countries imposed heavy taxes on the rich.[53] They concluded that inequality was not sufficient on its own to cause countries to impose high taxes. Instead, they found that raising taxes on the rich happened only when the public believed that the state had unfairly privileged the wealthy, such that higher taxes on the rich were necessary to compensate for that unfair advantage. These perceptions of unfairness were more likely in times of war, when working classes faced conscription while capital owners benefited from increased demand for their products.[54] Scheve and Stasavage argued that the reason progressive taxation saw its heyday in the United States in the twentieth century was because of these frequent conscriptions—first to fight two world

wars, and then again to fight the Korean War and the Viet-
nam War.[55] It is notable that the United States began cut-
ting taxes on the rich only after the draft was eliminated
in 1973.[56]

The circumstances surrounding the US entry in World
War I support a link between the military conscription of
men and the tax conscription of money. As the legal historian Ajay Mehrotra describes it, as American troops
began sailing overseas, "demands for the 'conscription of
wealth' to match the conscription of men began to fill the
editorial pages of the country's leading publications." Some
questioned whether taxes could even be sufficient: "The
Los Angeles Times rhetorically queried whether the minor
financial sacrifices made by the Rockefellers and the Fords
could compare 'with that of a man who bares his breast to
the bullets or the bayonets of the foe and risks his life for
his country.' "[57]

Congress raised the top rates for income and estate
taxes multiple times during World War I. But unlike earlier wartime financing measures that operated as tempo-
rary, these tax measures survived the return to normalcy
because their continuing revenues were used to create
popular expenditure programs. As the historian W. Elliot
Brownlee explained, "The popularity of the expenditure
programs, in turn, reinforced the popularity of the tax system behind the programs."[58]

Even so, with the ascent to political power by the industrialist Andrew Mellon—one of the wealthiest men in
America at the time, who also served as secretary of the

Treasury under the Republican presidents Warren G. Harding, Calvin Coolidge, and Herbert Hoover—the future of estate taxes was threatened as Mellon (unsuccessfully) sought their repeal multiple times.

Although Mellon opposed estate taxes, he did not deny the potential problems of inherited wealth. Rather, as Mellon claimed in his 1924 book *Taxation: The People's Business*, estate taxes were simply unnecessary to curtail inherited wealth: So long as the United States rejected primogeniture (and instead divided estates equally among children), wealthy dynasties would eliminate themselves through division and monetary mismanagement. In making his case, Mellon referred to the old Scottish proverb "Shirtsleeves to shirtsleeves in three generations"; that is, a generation of modest means, in shirtsleeves rather than a gentleman's coat, would create a fortune, their children would live in luxury and spend said fortune, and the third generation would find itself in the modest trappings of shirtsleeves.[59] While Mellon was ardent about this belief, his own family belied the phenomenon. In 2024, a century after Mellon published his book, *Forbes* still listed the Mellon family as one of the wealthiest families in the United States.[60]

The arrival of the Great Depression in 1929 caused even Andrew Mellon to change his tune. Amid a dire fiscal landscape, Mellon called for increases in estate taxes in the name of curtailing the rising federal deficit. The Republican Herbert Hoover, in his 1932 reelection campaign, also supported estate taxes, even expressly rebuking Mellon's old shirtsleeves maxim.[61] Sounding more like

Roosevelt than his prior self, Hoover said: "Luck and ge-
niuses create large fortunes. But the inheritance of great
economic power by descendants is not consonant with a
free people. We used to rely upon the incompetence of
the descendants to dissolve these accumulations. But the
old formula of shirt sleeves to shirt sleeves in three generations is impeded through the erection of two or three
generation trusts which are about as bad as the old law of
primogeniture."[62]

The Great Depression, like World War I before it, provided political impetus for the rapid and concerted expansion of the estate tax to help fill the nation's coffers. Between
1931 and 1941, the size of estates that were exempted from
the tax was lowered from $100,000 to $40,000; the initial
tax rate was tripled; and the top tax rate increased from
20 percent to a staggering 77 percent. Although the estate
tax had been adopted in 1916 to provide revenue for the
war, Franklin D. Roosevelt and his liberal New Deal coalition recast the estate tax as a means to fulfill the goals of
earlier progressives, including Theodore Roosevelt: Eliminating accumulations of inherited wealth would preserve
democratic ideals. "The transmission from generation to
generation of vast fortunes by will, inheritance, or gift is
not consistent with the ideals and sentiments of the American people," Roosevelt told Congress in 1935. "Such inherited economic power is as inconsistent with the ideals of
this generation as inherited political power was inconsistent with the ideals of the generation which established
our government."[63]

FDR's concerns surrounding inheritance and power were so great that in 1935 he proposed the adoption of an inheritance tax on those who *received* property, as a second tax on top of the estate tax. Roosevelt showed little patience for the rejoinder that this would destroy family businesses, arguing that the business itself need not be affected by the imposition of a tax. The economic and corporate principles, along with governmental protections such as patents, would all be unchanged: "All that are gone are the initiative, energy and genius of the creator—and death has taken these away."[64]

For decades after Roosevelt shepherded the New Deal state, the estate tax remained largely unchanged (save for adjustments to rates and exemption amounts) and remarkably consistent with the ideas espoused by Carnegie and Theodore Roosevelt before him. Its application was limited to the wealthiest 1–2 percent of Americans, who could avoid the tax altogether by donating their wealth to charity. Barring that, their transfers of wealth during life or at death were generally subject to estate taxes at significant rates, which ranged from 55 percent in 1942 to 70 percent in 2001.[65]

Of course, tax avoidance was not eliminated altogether. Some affluent families harnessed a new generation of complex trusts and tax-avoidance instruments to retain much of their fortunes. One of those families that was able to retain their wealth through the twentieth century and beyond was that of Franklin Mars, the American candy magnate. Mars started the company bearing his name in 1911, and more than a century later, the company has made the Mars heirs the second-richest family in America, with combined wealth of $117 billion in 2024.[66]

Among wealthy American families with recognizable names, few would think of the Mars family as arbiters of tax policy. Indeed, few would think of them at all: The Mars family have been referred to as a family that has "turned secrecy into a way of life."[67] (A running joke among residents of McLean, Virginia, is that the most secretive organization in their Washington suburb is not the Central Intelligence Agency, but Mars Inc.—the family's privately held confectionery and pet products company.[68]) With their passion for privacy, the Mars family was not happy about being listed among the *Forbes* magazine list of America's 400 wealthiest individuals. When Jacqueline Mars found herself seated at a dinner party near the magazine's editor, Malcolm Forbes, she threatened to leave the party if the hostess did not switch her to another table.[69]

And still, as much as the Mars family values privacy, their actions suggest they value something else even more: not paying taxes. In that area, they have not hesitated to put their considerable wealth toward achieving that end, even at the risk of becoming the public face of the movement against the estate tax.

THE DEATH OF TAXES

In 1991, Bill Clinton campaigned for the presidency to the tune of Fleetwood Mac's "Don't Stop," a song that encouraged people to dream about a better tomorrow. At the same time, several of the country's wealthiest families were doing just that. Specifically, the wealthy heirs of the Mars, Gallo, Walton, Koch, and other superrich families of America were dreaming about a tomorrow in which there would be no estate tax. Their actions at the end of the twentieth century would prove wildly consequential in the decade that followed.

As people who didn't need to work, the richest heirs in America were already treated very well under the income tax code. Unlike those with jobs, who pay both income and payroll taxes, individuals who live off inherited wealth are not similarly burdened. They receive their gifts and inheritances free from income tax, and they are often able to avoid tax on their investment gains by simply maintaining (i.e., not selling) ownership of their stock and other property interests until they die (when all gains are washed away). If they need cash, they can always get it through tax-free borrowing against their assets. And if they need, or want, to sell their investments, those gains are taxed at special reduced rates.

The only real tax obstacle facing these heirs, then, was the estate tax, which in the early 1990s was imposed at a top rate of 55 percent. What made this tax particularly troublesome for rich taxpayers was how, even as estate planners came up with clever workarounds, Congress kept shutting them down. At the end of the twentieth century, Congress had been particularly effective and comprehensive in its efforts.

For example, a popular technique at the time for wealthy families seeking to reduce their estate tax liability was to create long-term multigenerational trusts (the "two or three generation trusts which are about as bad as the old law of primogeniture" that Hoover railed against in his reelection campaign). These trusts were subject to tax upon their creation but not thereafter, allowing growing wealth to pass tax-free from one generation to the next. However, in 1976 and again in 1986, Congress significantly limited the power of this popular technique by adopting a new tax—the generation-skipping transfer tax—that served as a backup to the estate tax to ensure that a tax was levied at each generation regardless of whether property passed outright or in trust.[70]

Another popular technique developed by estate planners to reduce clients' tax liabilities was to manipulate the value of their estates by using trusts, partnerships, and limited liability corporations to shrink the value of ownership interests just long enough for them to pass from one generation to another.[71] Here again, in 1990, Congress stepped in to close the loophole by passing four new sections of the tax code, known as the special valuation rules, which significantly limited people's ability to game valuation through these techniques.[72]

These loophole-closing reforms were particularly concerning to the rich because the laws were enacted not at the behest of activist liberals, but under the leadership of the Republican presidents Ronald Reagan and George H. W. Bush.

For the wealthy, something needed to be done to make the estate tax as easily avoidable by rich heirs as the income tax. But given the broad bipartisan acceptance of the estate tax, they faced limited options. The most likely option available to them would be to seek an increase in the exemption amount, the amount that could be passed free of tax (at the time $600,000). This amount had been periodically increased over the years, typically to adjust for inflation; however, an increase of the exemption amount—no matter how generous—would not put a dent in the estate tax liability for these wealthy families, whose wealth was measured in the hundreds of millions, and even billions, of dollars.

The wealthy needed a bigger win—something audacious, something that had not been attempted since the days of Andrew Mellon. That was the moon shot they set out to achieve: full repeal of the estate tax.

With Democrat Bill Clinton taking the office of the presidency, 1992 might have seemed an inauspicious time to begin a campaign to cut taxes on the rich. But those attuned to the subtleties of political winds had reason for optimism, as Bill Clinton was not a typical Democrat.

For much of the twentieth century, Democrats had been associated with the politics of the New Deal—a belief that strong government had to constrain the harsher aspects of capitalism, including through the imposition of high taxes. The legacy of the New Deal had been so dominant that even a Republican like President Dwight D. Eisenhower had felt compelled to embrace its principles.[73]

But beginning in the 1980s, especially with the ascendancy of President Ronald Reagan, the politics of the New Deal began to give way to a new political trend, later termed *neoliberalism*: the belief that governments had to unshackle businesses from regulation in order for their economies to thrive.[74]

At first, neoliberal ideas were mostly associated with the Republican Party. But as the historian Gary Gerstle described in *The Rise and Fall of the Neoliberal Order*, Reagan's 1984 trouncing of New Deal Democrat Walter Mondale frustrated Democrats, who in turn began to reconsider their association with New Deal principles. Calling themselves Third Way Democrats, a group of Democratic politicians formed the Democratic Leadership Council (DLC) to shift the mission of the Democratic Party to align more closely with the interests of business—in the words of the DLC's Statement of Principles, "to expand opportunity, not government." The chair of the DLC in 1990 was none other than the Arkansas governor—later America's first neoliberal Democratic president—Bill Clinton. While Clinton did not himself support repealing the estate tax, as a Third Way Democrat he was sympathetic to the plights of business and the burdens of government. As such, he promoted an ethos that would provide fertile soil for messaging on repealing the estate tax to take root.

Against this landscape, as wealthy heirs planned their assault on the estate tax, they knew they needed to do two things: change the message and change the messenger. For the latter, they turned to the Republican pollster Frank

Luntz, known as "America's top political wordsmith." Luntz famously observed that "80 percent of our life is emotion, and only 20 percent is intellect," and "to get people to change what they think, you need to change what they feel."[75] Luntz played a central role in the seemingly impossible task of making average Americans care about a tax that applies only to a tiny sliver of the population—and only when they die.

The public relations problem with the estate tax, according to Luntz, began with the words commonly used to describe it: *estate* and *inheritance*. Neither one made people feel like they should care about its repeal. As Luntz wrote in his book *Words That Work*, "*Estate* conjures up images of rolling green hills and vast real estate holdings of J. R. Ewing"—the fictional patriarch of the 1970s show *Dallas*—"and Donald Trump rubbing their hands together and cackling like corporate villains or toasting with champagne glasses." *Inheritance*, meanwhile, evokes "images of celebrity debutantes, like Paris Hilton squandering the fruits of their parents' labor while the huddled, deserving poor tremble in the shadows."[76]

Through polling, Luntz found that the word *death*, particularly when combined with the word *taxes*, had a very different impact from the alternatives. On their own, *death* and *tax* are each a highly emotional word that produces lots of negative feelings. And the grim-sounding combination, *death tax*, sounded like something that applied broadly and was to be avoided at all costs. As Luntz later wrote, "While a narrow majority of those polled would repeal the inheritance/estate tax, an overwhelming majority would repeal the death tax." In other words, "if you want to kill the estate tax, call it a death tax."[77]

Once the rich had the message, they needed to change their messenger; tax reform measures would be difficult to secure using their own names. As much as Americans loved Snickers and M&M's, it would likely be a heavy lift for billionaire siblings Jacqueline and John Mars (the richest individuals in Virginia and Wyoming, respectively), to make the case directly to the public that their children should receive their inheritances free of taxes. To succeed, the rich heirs needed to remain hidden from public view and also provide a plausibly distorted view of who was actually subject to the tax. As Michael Graetz and Ian Shapiro explain in *Death by a Thousand Cuts*, the wealthy heirs seeking repeal knew they could only win popular support if the public could empathize with those seen as being vulnerable to the death tax; the working rich, not the idle rich, had to become the poster children of the movement.[78]

Supporters of repeal worked to ensure that the public would see the estate tax as an issue for small and medium-size businesses. To that end, proponents of the repeal put together a virtual rainbow coalition of business owners—Black, Hispanic, gay, women—all telling the same story: We are hardworking businesspeople just trying to live the American dream, and we are very worried about the government snatching our businesses away when we are at our most vulnerable—at death. (Whether these worries were based on reality was another matter: most of these small business interests were well under the exemption amount.)

The most effective of these spokespeople was Chester Thigpen, descended from enslaved Black grandparents and a third-generation tree farmer from Montrose, Mississippi. Thigpen testified to Congress in 1995 about his fears regarding the estate tax, recounting a vivid and powerful story about how he worked his land, plowing behind a mule, to create a beautiful tree farm with ponds, forests, and wildlife where children came to play and neighbors came to hunt. The farm produced enough income for him and his wife to send their five children to college. But Thigpen was worried that it was all about to come crashing down, afraid that the government would impose such heavy taxes when he died that his children would be forced to sell the farm for timber.

Chester Thigpen and his tree farm became the face of efforts to repeal the estate tax. In the 1998 report *The Economics of the Estate Tax*, Congress's Joint Economic Committee used Chester Thigpen's tree farm to illustrate "the burdensome nature of the estate tax" and to argue for the tax's repeal.[79] In the congressional debates over the tax, Chester Thigpen was mentioned dozens of times—not just as evidence of government overreach but as something greater: a victim of social injustice.

Thigpen's fear of the estate tax was actually unfounded, and he was not at risk of losing his farm to the estate tax. When Thigpen died, the land's value was far below the amount that would be subject to estate taxes. And even if the value had exceeded that amount, Thigpen's estate would have qualified for provisions that alleviated the estate tax burden for individuals inheriting family farms and businesses, including provisions for long-term payment plans with below-market interest rates for payment of any obligations that may be imposed. (Indeed, the availability of these provisions was one reason proponents of repeal had such a hard time finding actual families who had lost their farms to the estate tax.)

Although Thigpen was mistaken about whether he was subject to the estate tax, it is easy to understand the source of his fears. Supporters of repeal had spent millions of dollars in an advertising campaign designed to convince the public that the estate tax—like death—came for everyone (rather than a tiny sliver of the population) and that family farms and businesses were the main targets.

One $7 million advertising campaign ran this advertisement: "When you die, the IRS can bury your family in crippling tax bills. It can cost them everything." The ad was later criticized by FactCheck.org, an independent watchdog run by the Annenberg Public Policy Center for presenting a "misleading picture of who is actually affected by the estate tax since the vast amount of families are not affected by the estate tax." The media campaign was particularly fierce and misleading when it came to family farms and businesses. According to one ad: "The death tax is killing American businesses. . . . To pay the death tax, many are forced to sell."[80]

It is striking that this campaign was so effective considering that it was based on such blatant distortions of the truth. Opponents of the estate tax repeal had written their own reports and op-eds explaining the limited application of the estate tax and the protections—real and potential—for family farms and businesses. These received little attention.[81] To this, Luntz had a theory. As he explained in a *New Yorker* interview with Nicholas Lemann: "If you introduce a subject using language that will produce a strong opinion, no subsequent information will get people to change their minds. This is particularly the case when the competing claim is based on numbers—like in the estate tax where opponents of reform argued about lost revenue, high exemption amounts and the small percentage of the public likely to be subject to the tax. But discussing numbers is never a winning strategy." Describing politicians who talk about numbers, Luntz added: "It's like quicksand; the more you struggle the deeper you sink."[82]

In addition to the effective campaign, one aspect of this tax made it more vulnerable to challenge: The tax was designed as an estate tax (nominally imposed on the dead person giving the property) rather than an inheritance tax (imposed directly on the person receiving the property). The economic effect of estate taxes and inheritance taxes is similar: The person receiving the inheritance gets less because of taxes. However, framing the tax as a tax on the decedent, as opposed to the heir, makes it more vulnerable to the "death tax" and "double tax" framings. It's why supporters of the estate tax—including then senator Barack Obama—called it "the Paris Hilton tax"—to remind people who really benefits when we reduce estate taxes.[83]

The efforts of wealthy heirs to make repealing the estate tax a prominent issue succeeded beyond all expectations. Not only did they succeed in getting the Republican Party to adopt estate tax repeal on their party platform. President George W. Bush regularly brought up the importance of "eliminating the death tax" as a central talking point both during his campaign and after he was elected in 2000. Most importantly, the campaign to repeal the estate tax had a transformational effect on the way that average Americans viewed the tax. No longer did most Americans think of it as an innocuous tax on a small slice of the richest Americans. Rather, a significant portion of the public saw it as a death tax—and as an immoral double dip that hurt family farms and businesses.

JUBILEE; OR, A VERY GOOD YEAR TO DIE

Shortly after taking office in 2001, President Bush, aided by a Republican Congress, passed legislation that fulfilled his campaign promise of eliminating the estate tax ("death tax") at least for a bit. While Bush might have wished for immediate and permanent repeal, doing so would have carried a hefty political price tag, requiring him to make that amount up through budget cuts or other sources of revenue.[84] His only alternative was to limit the life of his legislation to ten years—and to hollow out the existing policy as much as possible.

To maximize his policy's impact across the ten years, and to fit existing budget constraints, Bush's tax plan provided for a gradual increase in the level at which estates were subject to tax (from $1 million in 2002 to $3.5 million in 2009), with a concurrent reduction in estate tax rates from 55 percent to 35 percent. Under the policy, 2010 would be a "jubilee year"—a total estate tax holiday for those, like the multibillionaire big-game hunter Dan Duncan, "lucky" enough to die that year. After that, in 2011 the law was to revert to where it was in 2001, like waking from a dream: a $1 million exemption threshold and a 55 percent tax rate.

Regardless of one's opinion on the issue of repealing the estate tax, there was broad agreement that this "here today, gone tomorrow, back again a year later" plan was one of the strangest things seen in the history of modern taxation. One widely noted concern was the incentives provided to the would-be heirs of those who might die in 2010, causing many to refer to the time as the "throw mama from the train" year, and prompting other clever quips, such as "gifts to get for your parents in 2010: hang-gliding lessons and warm chicken salad."[85] But it was all worth it for proponents of repeal, as the tax holiday served to further diminish the importance of the estate tax in the eyes of Americans, who were able to see that it was something the country seemed to be able to easily live without.

The long shadow of George W. Bush's tax jubilee extended to the presidency of Barack Obama. In 2011, when the estate tax was due to return to its pre-2001 state, many believed it would be allowed to return to the $1 million exemption and a 55 percent maximum tax rate, as provided under the 2001 tax law enacted under President Bush.

However, perhaps in recognition of the unpopularity of the estate tax, and with the hope of resolving the issue for family farms and businesses once and for all, Obama moved in the other direction. He removed 99.5 percent of Americans from the reach of the estate tax, increasing its exemption amount to $5 million per individual and $10 million per couple (to be adjusted for inflation) and capping the tax rate at 40 percent.

The Obama changes continued the trend of presidents reducing the reach of the estate tax. In 2000, before the Bush tax cuts were put into place, Americans filed 121,171 estate tax returns. Ten years later, the number had dropped to 47,320. Once Obama's tax plan went into effect, the number of estate tax returns dropped still further, to just 32,288 in 2013.[86]

If Obama believed he had resolved the estate tax issue, he was incorrect. In 2017, shortly after Donald Trump was elected, he signed into law sweeping changes to the tax code, including doubling the size of the estate tax exemption to $10 million per person adjusted for inflation. (In 2024, this exemption was $13.62 million per person.) The effect of the change was to further reduce the number of estates subject to the estate tax, from 32,288 in 2013 down to 6,158 (of which only 2,584 were taxable) in 2021. The effect of this change was that in 2001 the estate tax applied to 2.1 percent of decedents, but in 2019, the estate tax applied to only 0.07 percent of decedents.[87] Like George W. Bush, Trump was subject to the same ten-year budgeting restriction, meaning that his changes came with an expiration date at the end of 2025—at which point the envelope will most certainly get pushed further, particularly with President Trump back in power to carry forward his first administration's tax agenda.

While legislative changes increasing the exemption amounts and decreasing tax rates have served to undermine the effectiveness of the estate tax, far greater damage has come from Congress's failure to close its loopholes.

Even in its reduced state, the estate tax is still met with general antipathy. This is not just among Republican politicians who have long held estate tax repeal as one of their core platform positions. It is also true of many Democrats, who treat the estate tax like Voldemort in the Harry Potter series—a problem whose name must not be spoken.

An effective tax system isn't created in a one-and-done process; it's iterative. Congress first creates a set of rules, then taxpayers seek legal ways to circumvent them. This is an expected—and accepted—part of the system. As Justice Learned Hand famously wrote in 1934: "Anyone may so arrange his affairs that his taxes shall be as low as possible; he is not bound to choose that pattern which will best pay the Treasury; there is not even a patriotic duty to increase one's taxes."[88] However, if the goal is an *effective* tax system, this cannot be the end of the story. Taxpayers will always have financial incentives to find workarounds. If Congress stops doing its work, the system will fail.

In this way, tax-code writing is like computer programming. After its initial creation, a computer program is always subject to exploits that take advantage of its vulnerabilities. If we want the system to work, it must be constantly patched and upgraded. Expecting a tax system to work without continued congressional upkeep is like counting on Windows 95 to operate effectively in 2030—without updates.

For the first seventy-five years of the estate tax—from 1916 to 1990—this iterative system worked largely as intended, with Congress regularly revising the law to close loopholes.[89] But since 1990, members of Congress have engaged in a form of quiet quitting, sitting on their legislative hands while taxpayers and their advisers remain hard at work finding new workarounds. The names of these workaround techniques read like the secondary characters in a Dr. Seuss book: SLATs, GRATs and GRUTS, CLATs and CLUTs and CRATs and CRUTs, not to mention their cousins, NIMCRUTs and FLIPCRUTs. There are odd ones like Intentionally Defective Grantor Trusts and provocatively named ones like Dynasty Trusts (provocative because a stated purpose of the estate tax is to stop the creation of dynastic wealth). All of these are legal, and all are cleverly designed to undermine application of the estate tax. As Justice Hand suggested, taxpayers are perfectly free to exploit loopholes in the law, but Congress—like a diligent programmer—is supposed to close them.

For the wealthy heirs of America, this may be the best of both worlds. Although they did not win estate tax repeal, they may have won something better: explicit freedom from income taxes (which is sometimes justified on the basis of the existence of the estate tax), as well as a seemingly hidden freedom from estate taxes (which they can now achieve through some of the many available estate-planning techniques ignored by Congress). As a result, wealthy heirs enjoy the financial benefits of tax avoidance without bearing the reputational cost of public awareness. So long as the estate tax stands, even in its current moribund form, the wealthy can point to it to make the public *believe* that the wealthy are paying their fair share of taxes. If the estate tax were actually repealed, this shroud of decency would go with it.

Although efforts to permanently reform the estate tax remain underway—including the Death Tax Repeal Act introduced by Senator John Thune of South Dakota in 2025—the adoption of such a law would not necessarily be to the ultimate advantage of the wealthy. Without the distraction of the estate tax, the public might pay more attention to the ways the income tax gives a free pass to wealthy heirs on their investments and inheritances. Like the proverbial dog chasing the car, those seeking permanent repeal of the estate tax may be sorry if they catch it.

Meanwhile, today the United States is a country that bears all the trappings of an aristocracy, but the tax code and the changing optics of wealth and class provide significant cover. The brand of conspicuous consumption that Thorstein Veblen observed in the nineteenth century has given way to something better described as *stealth wealth*—rich people who look and dress and read their phones like anyone else, even as their political power and wealth have grown to unprecedented levels. The idea of America as a country where citizens share equal political power regardless of wealth or class—a principle so central to the country's founders—now resonates as quaint, even naive.

One of the reasons this system has been allowed to take root is that the American public has been led to believe that the wealthy are already carrying the lion's share of the tax burden while many Americans pay no taxes at all. A significant driver of this misunderstanding is the failure to recognize the role of payroll taxes. This is discussed in the next chapter, including how it is that payroll taxes have come to be so hidden from public view.

4

THE MYTH
OF NONPAYERS

In the summer of 2012 Senator Mitt Romney was in the midst of a heated presidential campaign against the incumbent, President Barack Obama, when he attended a $50,000-a-plate fundraising dinner at the Florida home of private equity manager Marc Leder. In what he thought was a private conversation with supporters, Senator Romney shared his perspective on the challenges of running against President Obama and his entrenched voter base. "There are 47 percent [of voters] who are with him, who are dependent upon government, who believe that they are victims, who believe the government has a responsibility to care for them," Romney said. "These are people who pay no income tax. . . . I'll never convince them that they should take personal responsibility and care for their lives."[1]

Unbeknownst to Romney, his comments were being videotaped and went viral soon after being published by the progressive magazine *Mother Jones*. Widespread criticism of Romney resulted, including from those in his own party. In response to the firestorm, Romney acknowledged that his comments were not "elegantly stated." But for several weeks, he declined to correct or retract the substance of his remarks, leaving in place the impression that nearly one-half of Americans were freeloaders who didn't pay any taxes.[2]

In one way, Romney was not wrong. At the time of his statement, 47 percent of Americans indeed did not pay any federal income tax.* But Romney's characterization of these Americans as nonpaying freeloaders who don't want to take responsibility for their lives was not just impolitic but inaccurate as well. One reason is that not paying federal income taxes is not a permanent status. It is common for Americans to experience times in life when they don't pay income taxes, either because they are in school, are serving in the military, are retired, or simply earn too little money. In addition, many of the country's wealthiest citizens are also nonpayers of income taxes when they live off their inheritances or borrow against their investments, two activities that generate no income tax liability.

However, the more fundamental problem with Romney's statement is that it ignores the fact that working individuals who don't pay federal income taxes still pay significant payroll taxes. And when you include payroll

---

* In 2024, the number was closer to 40 percent. This only refers to federal taxes; many of these individuals pay a slew of state taxes, including state income taxes, property taxes, and sales taxes.

taxes, the amount of people who truly pay no taxes falls to 16.5 percent—slightly less than the number of taxpayers who are older than seventy.[3]

The term *payroll taxes* might sound vaguely administrative and benign, but the effects of these taxes, both on a working person's finances and on the functioning of government, are hugely consequential. Payroll taxes are the second-largest source of federal taxes (after income taxes), accounting for more than a third of all federal revenue in 2024. Some 67 percent of taxpayers pay more in payroll taxes than in income taxes. For example, a self-employed person earning the median income of $60,000 in 2024 would owe only $4,677 in income taxes but $9,180 in payroll taxes.[4] Payroll taxes finance the country's largest programs: Social Security and Medicare. Over 97 percent of Americans expect at some point to receive benefits under these programs.

Payroll taxes appear different from income taxes because their funds come from a single source (wage and salary income), and they exist for the sole purpose of covering Social Security and Medicare. This framing leads many Americans to assume that payroll taxes are not taxes at all, but some form of employee savings in which money is collected and held in trust for the future. This perception is reinforced by the fact that they are referred to by the mysterious term *FICA contributions*, which makes it seem like they are gratuitous in nature.

Despite the terminology, payroll taxes are *not* contributions set aside for an individual's future; instead, they are taxes collected that are used to fund the benefits and medical expenses of current retirees and those with disabilities. In this way, payroll taxes operate like all other taxes: The government has a spending need, and it meets that need with a mandatory extraction of funds from taxpayers. For the taxpayer, that extraction is experienced as a tax like any other.

Senator Romney is not alone in ignoring payroll taxes. Indeed, while public conversations around taxes often focus on income taxes, corporate taxes, and estate and gift taxes, payroll taxes are typically left out of the equation. But how did a tax that raises so much revenue and funds such essential features of American society come to be so hidden from public view? The answer lies in the history of how we came to fund these expenses in the first place.

As some of America's wealthiest families spent the final years of the nineteenth century modeling their lifestyles after those of European nobility, a large swath of the country struggled simply to survive. The Panic of 1893 was the largest financial crisis in the short history of the United States, causing the closure of over fifteen thousand businesses and the loss of employment for one in four Americans. With virtually no federal or state programs in place to support them, and with charities and relief organizations unable to cope with the overwhelming demand, many saw the federal government (which had already provided support programs to veterans of the Civil War) as the only entity with the capacity to alleviate the desperate situation.

One person who looked to the federal government to address this crisis was Jacob Coxey, an Ohio businessman who, in the spring of 1894, led hundreds of men on a march from Massillon, Ohio, to the Capitol's steps for the country's first-ever march on Washington. These "petitioners in boots" sought to exercise their First Amendment right to "petition the Government for a redress of grievances" by asking the federal government to adopt a program to assist unemployed Americans. The extraordinary journey of the men in "Coxey's Army," who had traveled thirty-four days and more than four hundred miles on foot by the time they reached Washington, DC, was news in itself. But even bigger news was the kind of government policies they were marching to secure: a federal works program that would enable unemployed Americans to work on federally funded projects to support themselves and their families. The march dominated the press to such an extent that by the time it reached its final leg, thirty thousand people had lined the streets of Washington to witness, cheer, and in some cases join this first march on Washington.[5]

One Washingtonian who was not moved to lend support was President Grover Cleveland, who saw these requests for aid as solidly outside the responsibility of the federal government. The president's attitude was not surprising given his prior comments about the role of government. These comments were made in connection with a veto of a bill that would have provided grain to Texas farmers who were recovering from a devastating drought in 1887. While Cleveland acknowledged the aid would likely help the farmers avoid ruin, he nonetheless refused to support it: "I can find no warrant for such an appropriation in the Constitution. . . . [T]hough the people support the Government the Government should not support the people."[6]

With President Cleveland's opposition to federal assistance, the spectacle of Coxey's Army reached an ignominious end upon arrival in the nation's capital. No sooner had Coxey removed his speech from his jacket pocket than Capitol Police swept in with horses and billy clubs, dispersing the marchers and arresting Coxey for walking on the grass.[7] Coxey was fined $15 and jailed for twenty days. The pleas of Coxey's Army for public assistance—as well as those of more than a dozen other related marches by other unemployed workers across the country—went unanswered.[8]

Forty years after Coxey's march, in the throes of another financial panic (which President Hoover had called a "Depression" in an effort to make it sound less scary than the Panic of 1893), a newly elected Franklin D. Roosevelt had a very different response to the massive unemployment and financial insecurity of older Americans. Where Cleveland had regarded these issues as outside the scope of the federal government, Roosevelt saw them as quite the opposite: "If, as our Constitution tells us, our Federal Government was established among other things, 'to promote the general welfare,' it is our plain duty to provide for that security upon which welfare depends."[9]

Roosevelt's support for protective policies for the unemployed and those too old to work reflected the shifting needs of his time. As the US became industrialized, and as workers moved away from their families to work in cities, traditional sources of economic security—like extended family and close-knit communities—were less reliable. FDR emphasized this point in his 1934 address to Congress: "The complexities of great communities and of organized industry make less real these simple means of security. Therefore, we are compelled to employ the active interest of the Nation as a whole through government in order to encourage a greater security for each individual who composes it."[10]

FDR faced other pressures, too, not the least of which was growing public support for communism in the US, which was at an all-time high.[11] Meanwhile, other industrialized countries (including Great Britain, Germany, France, and Sweden) had recently developed their own programs to address financial needs of the unemployed and elderly, which further stoked the development of grassroots proposals in the US that were gaining support.

In response, a number of politicians proposed their own solutions to the problems of old age and unemployment. For Roosevelt, two that were particularly concerning were proposals from Upton Sinclair and Huey Long.

Sinclair, a journalist who authored the 1906 muckraking book *The Jungle*, exposing the harsh and unsanitary working conditions of the meatpacking industry, ran for governor of California in 1934 on the campaign message "End Poverty in California" (called EPIC). Sinclair called for the country to abandon capitalism and replace it with a cooperative socialist society. Although Sinclair ultimately lost the election, his ideas were very popular, and he garnered 37 percent of the vote in a three-way race.

Of greater concern for FDR, though, were the ideas proposed by Louisiana Senator Huey Long and his Share Our Wealth program, which he introduced to the public in a national radio address in February 1934.[12] Long's plan was to impose heavy taxes on the wealthy, with the proceeds to be distributed to Americans to provide them a basic estate (enough to buy a home) plus universal basic income, free higher education, a four-day workweek, and an annual pension for everyone over the age of sixty-five. Long's public coalition around Share Our Wealth had over 7.5 million members by 1935. Long was particularly threatening to Roosevelt because he planned to run against him as a third-party candidate in 1936 (he was expected to act as a spoiler, tilting the election to the Republican), and no doubt would have done so had he not been assassinated in 1935.[13]

While Sinclair and Long offered their plans as part of political campaigns, the plan that ultimately received the most attention—and came closest to any other to actually being adopted—had a far less auspicious beginning: a 1933 letter to the editor of a newspaper in Long Beach, California, written by a retired doctor named Francis Townsend. Townsend proposed a simple plan to address the financial needs of the elderly and fuel the economy: All Americans over the age of sixty who had stopped working would be given $200 at the beginning of each month, on the condition that they "take an oath to, and actually do spend, within the confines of the United States, the entire amount of their pension within thirty days after receiving the same."[14] Townsend proposed that his plan be paid for by a 2 percent sales tax collected by the federal government. While Townsend had no formal platform and no credentials to carry out his plan, support for the movement spread rapidly, first in California and then throughout the country, with millions joining "Townsend clubs." In just three months, twenty million Americans (one in five adults at the time) had signed petitions in support of the doctor's income-support scheme.[15]

Support for the Townsend plan was attributable in part to the success of Upton Sinclair's 1934 campaign for California governor. Against the popularity of Sinclair's EPIC proposal, the Republican candidate for governor, the incumbent William Merriam, was forced to provide his own solution to the economic problems of old age. To do so, he reluctantly threw his support behind the Townsend plan. By supporting a federal program, Merriam could meet his political needs without committing state funds.[16] Not long after Merriam's election, supporters of the Townsend plan had set up shop in Washington and begun their work lobbying Congress for its adoption.

The threat of these more radical plans, particularly the Townsend plan, prompted FDR to work quickly to develop his own plan.[17] In June 1934, he established the Committee on Economic Security, chaired by Secretary of Labor Frances Perkins, to craft a policy that would provide Americans "security against several of the great disturbing factors in life—especially those which relate to unemployment and old age." The most important thing to FDR was that the system be seen as one based on principles of social insurance, not welfare.[18]

It took only six months, until January 1935, for the Committee on Economic Security to introduce the legislation that established a national system for unemployment and old-age benefits. The critical question was, How should the program be funded?

The Commission on Economic Security proposed to Congress that the program be funded by a combination of contributions by employees (paid in the form of payroll taxes) and general federal tax revenue to make up any shortfall. However, this plan met with opposition from multiple sides.

The first to criticize the plan was Senator Huey Long, who objected to imposing any part of the cost of the program on workers. Long took to the radio two days after the bill was introduced to make his case, first, that it was inappropriate to impose taxes on working people and, second, that the only practical solution was to finance the program by taking money from the rich to give to the poor.[19]

Meanwhile, Roosevelt took the position that the whole program needed to be funded by workers, with no contribution through general federal funding. While Roosevelt was aware that taxes on payroll were regressive in nature—that they burdened poor people more than rich people—he justified a system based on workers' contributions as a way of arming the new system against political attack. As he later explained to a White House visitor who complained about the regressivity of the tax: "I guess you're right on the economics, but those taxes were never a problem of economics. They are politics all the way through. We put those payroll contributions there so as to give the contributors a legal, moral, and a political right to collect their pensions. . . . With those taxes in there, no damn politician can ever scrap my social security program."[20]

Roosevelt wasn't imagining things when he worried that Social Security would be vulnerable to political attack. In 1935, the idea of the government playing a role in the financial security of Americans was even more contested than it is today. One opponent to Roosevelt's policy was the broadcaster and journalist George Sokolsky, who was invited to offer a rebuttal to Frances Perkins's radio address explaining the newly proposed Social Security Act to the American public. Sokolsky described a Social Security program as nothing less than a step toward dictatorship, a means of social control. People would either have to "obey, or go to a concentration camp."[21]

In many ways, FDR's instincts were correct that a system structured as an insurance-like program funded by employee contributions would be more protected from political challenges. Since the system was enacted in 1935, Social Security has grown into an American institution, expanding in both coverage and scope (including with the establishing of Medicare in 1965). Today, Social Security affects the lives of more Americans than any other federal program—not just the aged and those with disabilities, but also their dependent survivors who receive death benefits. In 2024, sixty-seven million Americans—that's one in five—received Social Security benefits.[22] These resources help not only Americans who receive them but also businesses whose workers do not need to leave the workforce to provide for their elderly or disabled relatives and the economy as a whole: Greater economic security for individuals allows for more consumption, which fuels economic growth.

But Social Security is only insurance-*like*. If it operated like the insurance system FDR imagined (and like the one originally enacted in 1935), the system would have established large enough reserves to ensure the resources necessary to pay future claims. But that didn't happen, because soon after enactment, policymakers revised the law to give away the trust fund to early generations who had made only modest contributions.[23] As a result, instead of operating as true insurance, Social Security has operated largely as a pay-as-you-go system in which current workers support retirees through their payroll taxes.[24] Moreover, while the nation's intent is to provide future benefits for the aged and those with disabilities, workers do not have a legal right to their benefits. In 1956, Ephram Nestor, a Bulgarian immigrant, was deported from the US for his prior involvement—twenty years earlier—with the Communist Party. On top of his deportation, the government also stopped paying him his Social Security benefits, which he had paid into over the many years he worked in the US. Nestor sued for his loss of benefits. His case was ultimately decided by the Supreme Court, which held that

neither Nestor—nor anyone else paying into the system—
had a contractual or property right in retirement benefits,
and that Congress retained the right to change the rules as
it sees fit.[25]

The lack of protection for future retirees will have real
consequences beginning in the 2030s according to experts.
As aging baby boomers have created a historically high demand for retirement benefits, there has been no commen-
surate rise in contributing workers. The ratio of workers to
retirees has been declining for decades (from 5:1 in 1960 to
closer to 2:1 in 2024) and is expected to keep falling.[26] As a
result, the Social Security trust funds (used to supplement
payroll taxes to meet current demand) are due to run out
in 2035. Because the program is prohibited from paying
benefits without resources, benefits will need to be cut by
about 20 percent. To avoid across-the-board cuts, Congress must find ways to increase revenue, decrease selective benefits, or introduce some general tax revenue.[27]

Equally troubling, the language of *contributions* has
fostered a distorted sense among workers and the public
about who pays what. In the popular view, the 15.3 percent of wages that workers pay toward Social Security and
Medicare appears to be something other than a tax—even
while it absolutely is a tax. Those who are self-employed—
gig workers, freelancers, self-employed tradespeople and
professionals—feel the burden of payroll taxes most directly because they must pay the full 15.3 percent themselves and have to start filing returns with the government

after just $400 of earnings. But those employed by others are likely less aware of payroll taxes because, unlike income taxes, which require taxpayers to file annual returns, payroll taxes are collected and paid for by employers, without any filing or input from employees.[28] In addition, employees see only half of the payroll tax obligation coming out of their paycheck, with the other half being paid by their employer. However, most economists believe that employees ultimately bear the economic cost of the employer's share as well in the form of lower wages.[29]

Because payroll taxes are largely hidden, Congress has been able to increase their reach without much public outcry. Amid near constant pressure over the past fifty years to reduce the burden of taxes, Congress has responded accordingly—and selectively. From 1970 to today, the top income tax rate has fallen from 70 percent to 37 percent, and the top estate and gift tax rate has fallen from 77 percent to 40 percent. Meanwhile, over the same period, payroll taxes imposed on working Americans significantly *increased*, with tax rates more than doubling from 6.9 percent to 15.3 percent.

Unlike progressive income taxes, which increase as income increases, the payroll tax is highly regressive, meaning that it imposes significant costs on those with less income and fewer costs on those with greater income. Payroll taxes are collected starting with the first dollar earned and cannot be reduced through business expenses or other deductions.[30] This structure means that a freelancer with no children who earns $30,000 will still be required to pay over

$4,500 in payroll taxes.[31] In addition, payroll taxes are a true double tax because they are imposed on the full amount of earnings, even though some of those earnings are paid to the federal government in income taxes.

While payroll taxes impose real burdens on workers with low and moderate incomes, they are much less burdensome for individuals with high incomes. The bulk of payroll taxes—the 12.4 percent attributable to Social Security—applies only to the first $168,600 of wage income.[32] Thus, someone earning about $168,000 pays the same payroll tax as someone earning $1 million (there is no cap for the 2.9 percent Medicare tax).[33] And of course, those taxpayers who have income only from investments, like capital gains and dividends, pay no payroll taxes at all.

While the public is often told about the tax burdens borne by top earners, they are rarely told that the greatest government expense—payments for Social Security and Medicare—are borne almost exclusively by workers through their payroll taxes. In 2024, payroll taxes accounted for a full 35 percent of all revenue collected by the federal government, making them the most significant source of revenue after individual income taxes (which accounted for 49 percent of federal revenue). Payroll taxes also generate far greater revenue than corporate income taxes, which provided only 11 percent of total federal revenue, and virtually eclipse revenue from estate and gift taxes, which constitutes less than 1 percent of revenue.[34]

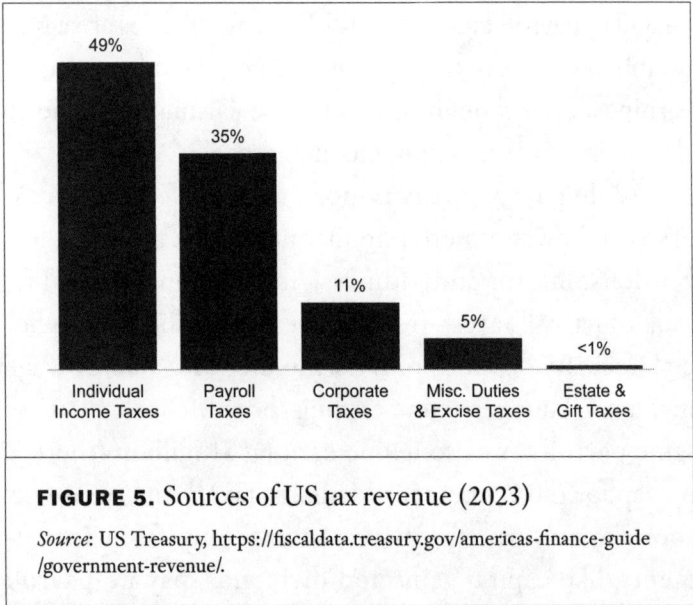

FIGURE 5. Sources of US tax revenue (2023)

Source: US Treasury, https://fiscaldata.treasury.gov/americas-finance-guide
/government-revenue/.

The payroll tax grew out of the need for Social Security, which grew out of the defining financial crisis of the twentieth century. As the next chapter shows, the twenty-first century's first major financial crisis prompted billionaires to be more proactive in protecting what's theirs.

5 THE *I* IN PHILANTHROPY

On March 24, 2009, with the United States in the midst of its largest financial crisis since the Great Depression, three billionaires sent letters to other billionaires around the country, inviting them to a secret meeting in New York City. The letters' recipients were undoubtedly accustomed to receiving invitations to exclusive events, but this one stood out for its notable signatories: Bill Gates and Warren Buffett, the two richest men in the country, and David Rockefeller, grandson of John D. Rockefeller and patriarch of one of the country's richest families.[1] The purpose of the meeting was to discuss "the worldwide recession and the urgent need to plan for the future."[2]

In the aftermath of the Great Depression, the United States imposed high taxes on the wealthy. These taxes remained in place for forty years, contributing to a period of wealth redistribution that was unprecedented in American history.

In 2009, as the country stared down a financial event of menacing scale, it would not be surprising if this group of twenty-first-century billionaires had this history on their minds.

If the billionaires believed a financial target was on their back, they weren't necessarily wrong. In 1982, *Forbes* began publishing an annual list of the four hundred richest Americans, including the specific net worth of each individual. American wealth was thus not only more transparent but also competitively ranked. During the financial crisis, the numbers that appeared on the 2008 list were staggering, especially in the context of a historic economic downturn. Gates and Buffett alone, at the first and second place atop the list, had combined wealth of over $100 billion. Together, the Forbes 400 together owned more than $1.5 trillion in wealth.[3]

The billionaires' first meeting produced no specific plan of action, but it was followed by several more dinners held across the country. In June 2010, these dinner discussions finally bore fruit. Buffett and Gates, along with Gates's then wife, Melinda French Gates, announced the creation of a new initiative, the Giving Pledge, whose purpose was to encourage the wealthiest Americans to commit up to 50 percent of their wealth to tackle "the most pressing problems of the world."[4] While these were not taxes, Bill Gates described the pledge as something loosely akin to a tax, claiming that the Giving Pledge would be a "mechanism for the redistribution of wealth."[5]

The pledge turned out to be less than promised. Unlike some charitable pledges, which can be legally binding, the Giving Pledge was designed to be "moral, and not legal" in its makeup—more of a pronouncement than a commitment.[6] Additionally, "the most pressing problems of the world" turned out to mean "whatever the donor wanted to do," even if that meant supporting their kids' private schools, or funding organizations whose purpose was to fight tax increases. Its freewheeling mission notwithstanding, the billionaire hedge fund manager Bill Ackman publicly declared that the Giving Pledge was truly the best of all possible worlds—an endeavor that the great social justice philosopher John Rawls would have lauded.[7]

Not everyone was as enthusiastic about the value of the pledge. Some questioned the optics of it, noting that the pledge resonated as "a PR thing, like they are royalty."[8] Others suggested it would be better for the rich to pay fair taxes and wages.[9] Some of the pledge's signatories were put off by the criticism, including Bernard Marcus, cofounder of Home Depot, who complained: "All this money is going for charity to help people—what kind of numbskull would find something wrong with that? Would they rather we bought yachts and built mansions?"[10]

The "yachts and mansions" defense is one of the most popular arguments in favor of billionaire philanthropy. In this telling, philanthropy is unassailably good because the philanthropist is giving away money instead of spending it on material goods. It is taken as a matter of faith that philanthropy is better for society than other things the wealthy could do with their money. But this view ignores the fact that philanthropy—unlike money spent on yachts and mansions—comes at a steep cost to the rest of us.

The US tax system provides generous tax benefits for wealthy charitable givers. Together, the charitable tax benefits that reduce income, capital gains, and estate and gift taxes can cut a wealthy donor's tax bill by up to 74 percent of the value of the donation.[11] This means that a donation of $100 million could generate up to $74 million in tax savings for the donor. Tax benefits for donors translate to forgone revenue for the federal government—revenue that would otherwise be available to be spent for the public benefit or to pay down the national debt or even to reduce tax burdens for others. Without tax benefits, the wealthy are giving away their own money; with tax benefits, they are giving away the American taxpayers' money as well.

This raises a question: What are American taxpayers getting for their investment? Because of the way the tax rules are written, the answer is: Often a lot less than we have been led to believe—and sometimes more than we bargain for.

AMERICA DEPENDS ON CHARITIES

Charities have always played a special role in the United States. This was observed by Alexis de Tocqueville, who, in his 1840 *Letters from America*, famously discussed the American tendency to turn to voluntary associations (the forerunner to today's charities) rather than government in seeking to better society: "Americans group together to hold fêtes, found seminaries, build inns, construct churches, distribute books, dispatch missionaries to the antipodes. They establish hospitals, prisons, schools by the same method. Finally, if they wish to highlight a truth or develop an opinion by the encouragement of a great example, they form an association."[12]

The American reliance on voluntary associations to fulfill essential social responsibilities—including aspects of education, health care, the arts, and basic social services—remains a distinctive feature of the country.

While these charitable organizations may receive some fees for services (like tuition or medical bills), as well as some direct government grants, much of their support comes from private charitable donations, incentivized and therefore indirectly funded by the federal government through the tax code.

Today's charitable sector operates as an essential cornerstone of current American society, employing about 10 percent of the American workforce and providing many services that would otherwise fall to government. Some charities doing this work, including some hospitals and elite universities, are multibillion-dollar enterprises that resemble businesses more closely than they do the voluntary associations of the nineteenth century.[13] However, the Tocquevillian ideal lives on through Americans across the country—in rural and urban settings—coming together to create voluntary associations to tackle society's most pressing problems in creative ways. At their best, charitable organizations promote civic engagement and address problems with a deeper understanding of the local community than could otherwise occur with top-down governmental programs. And on a macro scale, these organizations reflect the pluralism that is tied to the country's identity—an idea captured in the words of President George H. W. Bush when he referred to America's charities and volunteer efforts as providing "a brilliant diversity spread like stars, like a thousand points of light in a broad and peaceful sky."[14]

Charitable giving becomes *philanthropy* when wealthy Americans are the givers. In some cases, giving by the rich looks much like the charitable giving of other Americans, in that it is a donation given directly to a charity to help the charity fulfill its charitable mission. MacKenzie Scott, the philanthropist formerly married to Jeff Bezos, has become well known for this style of philanthropy, sending multimillion-dollar no-strings-attached grants to large and small charitable organizations throughout the country.[15] However, it is far more common for wealthy donors to retain control over their charitable donations by setting aside funds in private family foundations and donor-advised funds. These two giving vehicles work a little bit differently from each other, but they have one key thing in common: Donors can get immediate charitable tax benefits for setting funds aside while also deferring decisions on how and when the funds will be spent.

CHARITIES AND TAXES

Even though charitable organizations are independent from government, they still receive significant financial support at the city, state, and federal levels. Cities and other local governments exempt charities from property taxes on their real estate, states exempt them from sales taxes, and both state and federal governments exempt them from income taxes. But for many charities, the most important tax benefit is one that comes to them indirectly: tax incentives that encourage donors to make charitable donations.

The first incentive to encourage charitable giving was enacted in connection with the 1917 revisions to the income tax. The overarching purpose of the reforms was to generate revenue to fund the country's participation in World War I, and one way it did so was by significantly increasing the top income tax rate from 15 percent to a walloping 67 percent. Such a high rate on the wealthy's income concerned leaders from universities and other nonprofits, who worried that the higher taxes would make their donors less likely to make charitable donations. They convinced lawmakers that a reduction in donations would also result in Congress being forced to provide services otherwise covered by charities.[16] To balance the needs of charities and the federal government, Congress adopted the first income tax deduction for charitable giving, but it did so with a cap that allowed donors to offset only a small amount of their income (no more than 15 percent) with charitable donations. The limit on deduction served an important purpose: It ensured that charitable donations didn't undermine financing of the war effort, while still providing an incentive for donors to support charities. The same is true today: The charitable deduction for income taxes is subject to an annual limit, which prevents income earners—and just income earners—from completely eliminating their income tax liability through charitable giving.

Shortly after the adoption of the income tax deduction for charitable giving (including its annual limits), two more charitable tax incentives were added to the tax code—provisions that have been particularly valuable to wealthy Americans. The first allowed for the total avoidance of capital gains taxes when appreciated property is donated to charity.[17] The second allowed for unlimited estate tax and gift tax deductions when charitable donations are made during life or at death, including to a family foundation or a donor-advised fund.[18] These rules, which are still in effect, provide no limits on the use of charitable donations to offset capital gains taxes and estate tax and gift taxes, allowing the wealthiest Americans to completely eliminate these types of tax liabilities through charitable giving.

CHARITABLE DEDUCTIONS AS FEDERAL SPENDING

Charitable tax benefits have long been understood as a subsidy from the federal government to encourage donors' charitable giving.[19] So, if a donor gives $1,000 to the Red Cross and then claims the charitable deduction reducing this income tax liability by $300 (which would be the case if the donor was subject to taxes at a 30 percent rate), this is the same as if the donor pays $1,000 to the Red Cross, and the federal government turns around and sends $300 back to the donor; an alternative way of seeing this is that the $1,000 donation is funded with $700 by the donor and $300 by the federal government.[20]

The federal government refers to these as *tax expenditures*—money it spends through the tax code instead of through the normal budgetary process. To inform policymakers and the public about the full extent of these costs, each year the federal government is required to calculate and publish the cost of different tax expenditures in an annual tax expenditure budget. In 2024, the income tax charitable deduction alone cost the federal government $64 billion in forgone taxes.[21] But this cost most certainly pales in comparison to the forgone revenue from the tax benefits offsetting capital gains and estate and gift taxes.

Charitable tax benefits are typically defended on the grounds that they stimulate voluntary donations for the public good, including by reducing work that might otherwise fall to government. Although tax benefits can be expensive, if they induce donations that would not otherwise be made, they could be seen as a good deal; they allow the government to produce social good at a lower cost than if the government had to finance the whole thing itself. Applying the previous example, the tax incentive for the Red Cross contribution allows the government to produce $1,000 of disaster relief while paying only $300 for it. The rest came from a private citizen.[22]

These tax benefits are also framed as a way of promoting more diverse solutions to society's problems than can be achieved through direct spending for government programs.

This can be seen by looking at some of the myriad creative ways that different charities work to better the world, including through such diverse programs as theater arts programs for incarcerated adults, "baby kits" with essential supplies and information to support new mothers living in underserved communities, or backpacks filled with school supplies for kids starting school.[23] These are on top of the many traditional charities, like schools, churches, hospitals, and organizations engaged in scientific research or preventing cruelty to animals. The flexibility afforded charitable organizations is particularly valuable in a pluralistic society like the United States, where there is no shortage of social problems and many competing views about how best to solve them.

The law and economics scholar Saul Levmore defended charitable tax benefits as a way of ensuring that the government spends its resources in accordance with the wishes of its taxpayers. If the Red Cross is a preferred recipient of charitable dollars, the government will, at least in theory, effectively make larger matching grants to the Red Cross, as opposed to less-popular charities.[24]

But incentive programs achieve their purpose only if carefully designed—if the $300 tax benefit produces at least as much benefit to the public as it costs the federal government. If tax incentives aren't carefully crafted, they can end up reducing government revenue without producing the promised societal benefit. And for better or worse, when it comes to designing tax rules, there are many forces pushing for change that are not necessarily interested in promoting the public good.

CHARITABLE BENEFITS ARE CONFUSING, AND SOME BENEFIT FROM THE CONFUSION

Few things in the tax code cause greater confusion to the American public than the tax benefits of charitable giving. While Americans are well aware that charitable giving can produce tax benefits, they are far less aware of who gets them and how much they get.

The simple facts are that the vast majority of Americans receive zero tax benefits for their charitable giving while the wealthiest Americans enjoy multiple benefits, the sum of which can provide them—and cost the federal government—as much as 74 percent of the value of their donation.[25] Meanwhile, the public has been led to understand that the opposite is true: that regular Americans get lots of benefits and the richest Americans get hardly any. This confusion has been fueled by both charities and by the wealthy—each of which has its own interest in keeping the public confused about the true nature of tax benefits.

Charities have an interest in keeping the public in the dark about the fact that most taxpayers receive no tax benefit for their charitable giving. The lure of tax benefits is a primary driver of the donations that sustain charities. Nonprofits take advantage of this confusion by holding fundraising drives at the year's end, reminding people that they have only so many days left to take advantage of that year's tax benefits. What is not mentioned, and is therefore less well known, is that 90 percent of taxpayers receive no tax benefit—zero!—for their charitable giving. This deception leaves many Americans believing that they are getting far more benefits for charitable giving than they are. The tax scholar Lilian Faulhaber refers to this phenomenon as the *hypersalience of the charitable deduction*—a dissonance in which people believe that charitable giving equals tax savings, without understanding the limits or realities of the tax system.[26] Meanwhile public confusion around the availability of tax benefits remains, evidenced by the fact that a significant amount of charitable donations are made in the last three days of December.[27]

Just as charities benefit when the public fails to understand the limited availability of charitable tax benefits, the wealthy benefit when the public is kept in the dark about how extensive their charitable tax benefits really are. While 90 percent of taxpayers get no tax benefits for their charitable giving, the wealthiest enjoy multiple benefits by making well-planned gifts that save them not just income taxes, but capital gains and estate and gift taxes as well. Taken together, these benefits can be worth as much as 74 percent of the value of the donation. These extensive charitable tax benefits for wealth owners are rarely mentioned in public discourse around charitable giving, and some wealthy donors take advantage of this void by constructing false narratives about the extent of their benefits. Two of the most financially sophisticated members of this group,

Warren Buffett and Bill Gates, have issued recurring public statements that actively understate the tax benefits they've achieved from their charitable giving.

WHY MOST AMERICANS GET NO TAX BENEFITS FROM CHARITABLE GIVING

Regular working Americans receive little or no tax benefits for their charitable donations because of the kinds of taxes they pay. People who have to work for their money pay payroll taxes and income taxes, and those taxes provide little or no benefits for charitable giving.

For example, imagine that Anna, a self-employed architect, earns a $100,000 salary. Absent any charitable donations, Anna will owe payroll taxes of $15,300 and income taxes of $14,300, for a combined federal tax obligation of just under $28,000 ($27,900).[28] Now, what tax benefits will she get if she makes a $10,000 donation to the local food bank, even after she holds on to the receipt and keeps it handy as she's filing her taxes? Surprisingly, none. Her tax-deductible donation produced zero tax savings.

There are two reasons this happened to Anna. The first is that payroll taxes (which constitute more than half of Anna's tax liability) cannot be offset by charitable giving, or indeed by any other deductions. The second is that the rest of Anna's taxes are income taxes, which for 90 percent of all taxpayers provide no tax benefits for charitable giving. This has been the case since the first Donald Trump tax cuts of 2017 raised the standard deduction, which significantly reduced the number of Americans who can benefit from their charitable giving.

The reason has to do with an aspect of the income tax rules that few Americans understand: the difference between itemizing deductions and claiming the standard deduction. As many know, the tax code provides a variety of deductions that can be used to offset income, like the home mortgage interest deduction and the charitable deduction. However, to claim those deductions, taxpayers are required to maintain receipts and report—that is, "itemize"—each deduction on their tax return. To provide an optional alternative to this system, one that makes it easier for people to file their taxes, Congress enacted a "standard deduction" in 1944 that provides an alternative to itemizing—a standard amount that each taxpayer can claim as a deduction, with no supporting paperwork required. All taxpayers are allowed to choose between itemizing their deductions and claiming the standard deduction, but in practice, the decision is generally based on whether the total deductions are more or less than the standard deduction. Over the years the standard deduction has increased, thereby making it the more financially attractive choice for more and more taxpayers. The greatest increase occurred in 2017, when the standard deduction was doubled from $6,000 to $12,000. As a result of this increase, forty-five million taxpayers went from being itemizers (and getting tax benefits for their charitable giving) to taking the standard deduction (and getting none). Today the standard deduction is used by 90 percent of Americans. Those who itemize (and therefore get income tax benefits for their charitable giving) also tend to be those with the most income. In 2020, 45 percent of all charitable deductions were claimed by taxpayers earning more than $1 million (and a startling 28 percent were claimed by those earning more than $10 million). Meanwhile, only 15 percent of charitable deductions were claimed by those earning less than $100,000.[29]

Even earners who are big givers—such that their deductions are greater than the standard deduction—are still limited in their ability to offset income taxes. This is because, just like the first income tax charitable deduction adopted in 1917, today's income tax still caps the amount of income that can be offset by the charitable deduction each year.[30] Today that cap is between 20 percent and 60 percent of the taxpayers' taxable income, with the exact percentage dependent on the nature of the property donated and the type of charitable recipient.[31] This means that no matter how large of a charitable donation an earner makes, she will still not be able to eliminate her income tax liability through charitable giving.

To see how this works, let's go back to Anna, our self-employed architect earning $100,000 and owing about $28,000 in payroll and income taxes. Imagine that Anna wanted to give all of her $100,000 to the food bank. If she were to do so, she would still not be able to offset her payroll taxes. But since her deduction is so much larger than the standard deduction, she would itemize her deductions and, at least potentially, could offset her income taxes. However, due to the cap that limits the deduction for charitable giving, Anna's income tax deduction for her $100,000 donation would be limited to somewhere between $20,000 and $60,000. This means that she would still be paying income taxes on between $40,000 and $80,000 of her income that year, even though she gave all of her $100,000 in earnings to charity.

Although this cap may seem unfair, it was born of an important value in our tax system: Charitable giving is valuable, but so is supporting the expenses of government. The relevant question, then, is why this concern does not also apply to the wealthy.

WHY THE WEALTHY GET SO MANY TAX BENEFITS FROM CHARITABLE GIVING

The tax code has a systematic bias in favor of wealth owners instead of earners, and this bias extends to charitable tax benefits. While earners (those subject to payroll and income taxes) get little or no tax benefit for their charitable giving, wealth owners can often completely eliminate their capital gains and estate and gift tax liability through charitable donations. (These savings come on top of any available income tax benefits, which are capped in the manner just described.) Unlike the generally unavailable and always limited charitable tax savings for earners, charitable tax savings for wealth owners are generous and unbounded.

Earners usually overestimate the value of their tax benefits from charitable giving. Wealth owners tend to underestimate theirs—at least in their statements to the public. They do so by highlighting the limitations on their *income tax* benefits—which are capped for anyone with an income—and by failing to mention the tax benefits they enjoy by saving on capital gains and estate and gift taxes.

Two of the biggest purveyors of this misinformation are none other than two of our most famous philanthropists: Bill Gates and Warren Buffett. It is notable that when Gates and Buffett make statements about their respective finances—whether income, taxes, or philanthropy—the statements are not off-the-cuff responses to other people's questions. Instead, they are well-crafted personal financial narratives, provided voluntarily in public-facing documents.

The following Gates statement appeared as part of an FAQ on the Bill and Melinda Gates Foundation website in 2024 (reproduced here in its entirety):

QUESTION: Do Bill and Melinda get tax breaks for their donations to the foundation?

ANSWER: Many individuals enjoy tax benefits as a result of making charitable contributions. The amount of tax savings received depends on both the size of the charitable contributions and the person's annual income.

Bill and Melinda have been exceptionally generous in making contributions to the foundation, donating sums much larger than their annual incomes. As a result, the tax savings they receive from these contributions represent a very small percentage of the contributions.

From 1994 through 2018, Bill and Melinda gave the foundation more than $36 billion. *Those donations resulted in a tax savings of approximately 11 percent of the contributions they made over that time.*[32]

Here, "tax savings of approximately 11 percent of the contributions they made" likely reflects the *income tax* savings on those $36 billion in donations. But the answer fails to account for other, far more substantial tax benefits the Gateses enjoyed, including avoiding 20 percent capital gains taxes that they would otherwise pay on the disposition of highly appreciated Microsoft stock and a 40 percent savings on what they would have paid in estate and gift tax had they not been able to take advantage of the unlimited charitable deduction. Combined, Bill and Melinda Gates's tax savings from their donation to the Gates Foundation was closer to 70 percent, not 11 percent.

Warren Buffett took a similar approach when describing the tax benefits that he received from his charitable donations. In a 2021 report, Buffett said: "In my own case, the $41 billion of Berkshire shares I have donated to the five foundations has led to only about 40 cents of tax savings per $1,000 given. That's because I have relatively little *income*."[33] Like Gates, Buffett focuses on income tax savings, leaving out his other, massive savings on capital gains and estate and gift taxes—taxes that would apply were he to sell his stock or bestow the property to his kids. Because of the unlimited charitable tax benefits, capital gains and estate and gift tax savings would provide between a 40 percent and 60 percent tax benefit for Buffett (costing American taxpayers as much as $24 billion in forgone revenue on his $40 billion donation). This is in addition to the income tax benefit of less than .005 percent that he claims.

Buffett maintains that this is best for all involved—that his charitable giving is better than if he had paid taxes: "I believe the money will be of more use to society if disbursed philanthropically than if it is used to slightly reduce an ever-increasing US debt," he said.[34] Buffett's opinion, like his accounting, leaves unanswered questions. One important one is, Why does he get to choose?

THE COSTS OF CHARITABLE TAX BENEFITS

How much are we forgoing in tax revenue for all this charitable giving? Unfortunately, we can't know for sure, because the reported information is disturbingly scant.

Since the 1970s, Congress has tried to bring more transparency to the real cost in forgone tax revenue stemming from different tax provisions through its tax expenditure budget. The problem is that, when it comes to charitable tax benefits, the public only gets the information about the costs of the income tax deduction, and not the costs of the forgone capital gains taxes or estate and gift taxes.

In 2024, the loss of revenue from the income tax deduction alone was $64 billion. However, since the income tax charitable deduction is available to only a small number of itemizing taxpayers, and because it is also subject to an annual cap, the forgone revenue from the loss of capital gains and estate and gift taxes is far greater than the loss of revenue from the income tax. How much do these other tax benefits cost the federal government in forgone revenue? Here it is anybody's guess. But it's a *lot* more than $64 billion.

The absence of information is particularly troubling as it relates to the unlimited charitable deduction for estate and gift tax purposes. For the wealthiest Americans, this is the most significant tax they face, as taxable income is easy to avoid for those who rely on investments and inheritances. Once having passed the exemption amount ($13.62 million in 2024), a 40 percent tax is imposed on all wealth transfers made during life or at death. This also means that each dollar eligible for the tax deduction costs the federal government forty cents in forgone revenue. Across thousands and thousands of deductions by millionaires, centimillionaires, billionaires, and centibillionaires, the forgone tax revenue quickly adds up.[35] Until 2003, the federal government tracked and published the cost of this deduction. However, in 2003, as part of President George W. Bush's attempt to eliminate—and delegitimate—the estate and gift tax, he ordered the Treasury to stop collecting and publicizing tax expenditures associated with the estate and gift tax.[36] The result has been a critical loss to the public in terms of providing accurate, official information about the true cost of philanthropy.

What we can know, however, is that the scale is big. Every billion dollars donated provides at least $400 million in savings on the estate and gift tax. For centibillionaires like Gates and Buffett, who have publicly proclaimed that they will give away all their wealth, the value of the tax benefits is of a different order: $40 billion for each $100 billion given away. And as the saying goes, "$40 billion here and $40 billion there and soon you're talking about real money."[37]

If capital gains and estate and gift tax benefits were subject to the same overall limitation for charitable giving that applies for income tax purposes, then donors would still be incentivized to make charitable donations—even of their entire estate—but they would also be required to join the rest of us in supporting the costs of government.

WHAT DO WE GET FOR OUR INVESTMENT IN CHARITABLE GIVING? SOMETIMES NOTHING

When Congress first adopted incentives for charitable giving in 1917, it did so to encourage donations to universities, hospitals, churches, food banks, and other organizations involved in providing charitable services. To ensure that these charities got the funds they needed, the rules tied the tax benefits to donors giving up "complete dominion and control" over their donated funds. After all, it was only when a charity had full control over the funds that it could put those funds to use.

In the intervening years, a structural shift occurred that broke the connection between charitable tax benefits and benefits to charities: the rise of private foundations and donor-advised funds. These organizations typically do no charitable work themselves but simply hold funds for future charitable distribution. Private foundations and donor-advised funds allow donors to get the full tax benefits of charitable giving when they contribute funds, but they provide no meaningful obligation for the funds to ever be spent.

In 2024, over $1.7 trillion was set aside in private foundations and donor-advised funds, awaiting instructions from donors and providing fees for money managers.[38] Meanwhile, charities—and taxpayers who partnered in the creation of these funds—have no assurances that the funds will ever put to use for society's benefit.

This is not by design, but by regulatory failure. The rules on the books are designed to ensure that tax-benefited dollars make their way to working charities. However, congressional inaction in this century has allowed wealthy taxpayers to exploit a loophole that threatens to undermine the integrity of the whole charitable tax system. By permitting the "deduct now, donate later" donor-advised funds, Congress severed the connection between charitable giving and giving to charity, not just for donor-advised funds, but for private foundations, too.

The Changing Forms of Philanthropy

Charitable tax benefits in the US were established to encourage donors to support organizations that benefited people's lives and help fulfill needs that would otherwise fall to government. However, as tax rates rose in the first half of the twentieth century, tax lawyers and their clients came up with a way to claim charitable tax benefits without actually giving money away: They created their own personal "charities" (later termed *private foundations*), providing them a tax-free vehicle for running their businesses and lives, all without paying taxes. While some of this money might have gone to charitable ends, it did so only at the whim of the donor and not as the result of any legal rules that required that result.[39]

Congress was skeptical of the value of these private foundations. In the 1960s, it considered a variety of alternatives that would have ended, or at least significantly curtailed, their existence, including limiting the life of private foundations to twenty-five years.[40] Instead, in 1969, Congress adopted a tax regime that added benefits for contributions to public charities and impose greater restrictions on private foundations. The goal was to end abuses on tax deductions and to ensure a closer connection between the tax benefits afforded to donors and the charitable benefit to the public.

The central feature of the legislation was its differentiation of *public charities*, which received donations from the public to do charitable work (organizations like schools, churches, food banks, the Red Cross, and the myriad other organizations formed to address society's problems) from private foundations. The latter were defined as charitable organizations, created and funded by a small number of people in order to fund charitable work typically done by others. Congress sought to get more money to the public charities—the organizations doing the charitable work—while imposing greater oversight on private foundations to ensure that they were in fact providing a public benefit.

To direct more money to public charities, the 1969 tax legislation provided greater benefits for donations to public charities than to private foundations. More consequentially, the legislation also imposed a set of rules to ensure that private foundations were actually providing for the public benefit—not, as was sometimes the case, existing as a mere mechanism by which an individual could move money from one donor-controlled pocket to the other in order to receive a tax benefit.

To that end, the legislation imposed an array of new rules on private foundations. One, called the *payout rule*, requires foundations to pay 5 percent (originally 6 percent) of their assets each year to charitable endeavors. Another required the foundations to disclose information to the public about where they get their money and how they spend it, which in turn allows journalists, researchers, and the general public to monitor whether they are serving the public good.

In an ideal world, these rules would have encouraged greater donations to organizations doing charitable work while providing greater assurances that private foundations would benefit the public. However, as often occurs in tax law, no sooner were meaningful rules put in place than the seeds of their avoidance were planted and harvested. In 1969, the seeds were planted by Norman Sugarman, a Cleveland tax lawyer. As the historian Lila Corwin Berman wrote: "If you asked most people why the year 1969 was important in American life, few would mention that year's federal Tax Reform Act. But Norman Sugarman's fingerprints on that document may have had as much of a lasting effect on this country's history as Neil Armstrong's feet on the moon."[41]

Sugarman represented several community foundations in Cleveland, Ohio, that served to connect wealthy donors to charitable organizations in the community. With the changes from the 1969 legislation, Sugarman recognized that the new regulations could either crush his clients or provide them with a windfall. He found a way to accomplish the latter. The first step was to establish public charity status for the organizations he represented, enabling them to avoid the limitations of tax benefits and oversight imposed on private foundations. He then developed a mechanism by which wealthy donors could use a community foundation as a sponsor for the donors' charitable giving. This arrangement, called a donor-advised fund (or DAF), allowed donors to reap all the benefits of an immediate outright gift to a public charity (the same they'd receive for giving money outright to a food bank or other public charity) while effectively maintaining ongoing control over the investment and its subsequent charitable distributions.[42]

The key behind the new arrangement was that it functioned in a legal gray area: If the donor retained actual legal control over the charitable distribution of the funds in a DAF, no deduction would be allowed. But because donor-advised funds relied on a wink-and-nod understanding, the donors would sign a statement that they were giving up full control over the donation to the community foundation, thus securing immediate tax benefits. The quiet understanding, in turn, was that the community foundation would not spend the money itself but would instead set it aside in a separate account, awaiting charitable spending instructions from the donor. In the wake of the 1969 tax law, the donor-advised fund provided an alternative for people who wanted the current tax benefits and ongoing control they got through giving to a private foundation, but without the hassles of conforming to all the new rules.

The Thing That Ate Philanthropy

When they first emerged, donor-advised funds were relatively small players in the charitable landscape. That changed in 1991, when Fidelity Investments, one of America's largest investment companies, announced it was creating its own "charity"—Fidelity Charitable—which would operate solely for the purpose of sponsoring donor-advised funds.

From a business perspective, it was a brilliant move. Fidelity's business was money management, and the more money it managed, the more revenue it generated. By creating its own "charity," Fidelity offered its clients the ability to get up-front charitable benefits while maintaining control over the investment and charitable distribution of the funds. In the meantime, the money "donated" to Fidelity Charitable often remained invested in Fidelity's investment accounts, earning fees for Fidelity money managers. Fidelity quickly rose to one of the top 20 charities in the US, and in 2015, it became the largest charity in the United

States by dollars raised, surpassing United Way and the Red Cross.

Soon after Fidelity created Fidelity Charitable, Charles Schwab and Vanguard Investments, both financial services companies, followed suit, creating their own DAF sponsors, Schwab Charitable and Vanguard Charitable. The marketing of DAFs by financial institutions also served to increase the popularity of DAFs sponsored by community foundations, including one of the largest servicers of the tech industry, the Silicon Valley Community Foundation. Of the top twenty charities that received the most charitable donations in 2021, more than half were DAF sponsors.[43]

Donor-advised funds rose to prominence in response to the 1969 legislation. A half century later, they had successfully gutted the legislation's intended reforms. The effects have been multiple. First, the purpose of the public charity status designation was to direct more money to organizations engaged in charitable work and less money to private foundations. From the donor perspective, DAFs made this difference between public charities and private foundations less relevant. A DAF donation provides donors with all the tax benefits of an outright donation to a public charity without surrendering control. But because there are also no payout obligations with DAFs, there is no certainty that the money will ever be spent on charitable ends.[44]

Second, DAFs undermine the federal regulation of private foundations. Private foundations still technically have a 5 percent payout rule, but foundations can meet the letter of the law—while avoiding its purpose—by simply transferring their required 5 percent payout to a DAF, thereby retaining functional control over the money.

Third, DAFs allow private foundations to avoid the public scrutiny that Congress wanted them to have. If a private foundation makes a direct donation to a hate group or other questionable charity, that information is available to the public through public disclosure of tax returns. But if the private foundation wants to avoid this disclosure, it can simply make a distribution to a DAF, then make the donation to the hate group from the DAF, and no one is the wiser.[45] While DAFs do publish their distributions, they list them over thousands of pages, and the information is disconnected from any particular donor.

Finally, using a DAF can undermine the whole division between private foundations and public charities. If a donor gives $100 million to his own newly created donor-controlled charity, that charity will be a private foundation, subject to lesser tax benefits and to payout and disclosure rules. But if the same donor gives the same contribution to a DAF and then makes a distribution from the DAF to the same newly created charity, the newly created charity is now a public charity; the government treats the donation as coming not from the donor but from another public charity (the DAF sponsor).

These perverse dynamics are well understood by experts and professionals who work in philanthropy and advise donors, but to date they have proved difficult to address with new legislation. One measure of bipartisan legislation from 2021, the Accelerating Charitable Efforts (ACE) Act, proposed closing these loopholes and restoring the purposes and

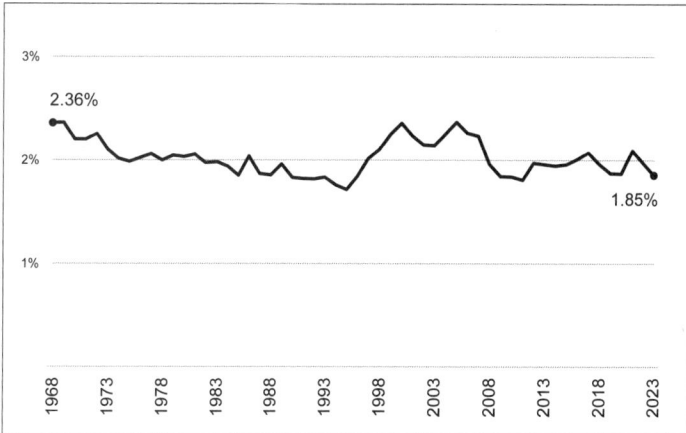

FIGURE 6. Individual giving as a share of disposable income (1983–2023)

Source: Individual giving data from Giving USA. Personal disposable income from Bureau of Economic Analysis, "Personal Income and Its Disposition," seasonally adjusted at annual rates (current dollars).

strength of the 1969 rules.[46] However, under intense lobbying by sponsors of donor-advised funds, the legislation didn't pass.

As private wealth has grown, and amid bold pronouncements of philanthropic largesse like the Giving Pledge, one might expect charitable giving to have increased in recent decades. It has not. From 1968 to 2023, total charitable giving has remained remarkably consistent: about 2 percent of disposable personal income (defined as that which is available after taxes have been paid).[47] Indeed, to the extent that there has been any change since the time of the Giving Pledge, it has been downward, as total giving in 2023 was at the historically low rate of 1.85 percent of distributable income.

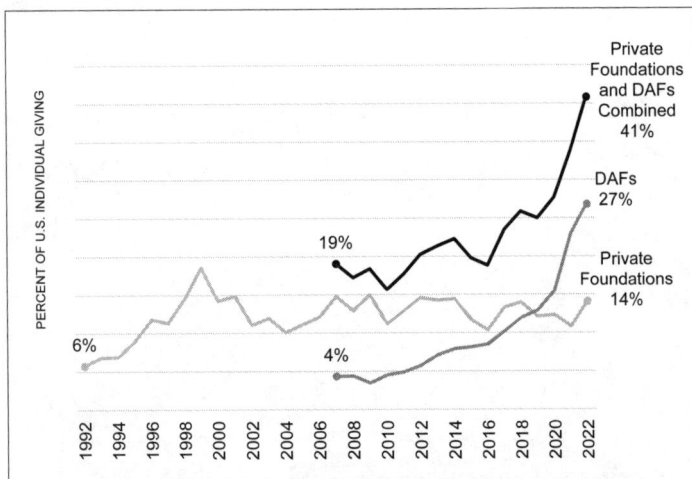

FIGURE 7. Percentage of US individual charitable giving going to private foundations and donor-advised funds

Source: Institute for Policy Studies analysis of data from the National Philanthropic Trust and Giving USA.

Note: Foundation giving is from Giving USA, minus the amount the National Philanthropic Trust reported as given to community foundation donor-advised funds (to avoid double-counting that revenue). Donor-advised fund revenue was not tracked until 2007.

While the inflow of charitable donations has stayed the same, the places these donations go have changed dramatically. In 1993, 94 percent of all charitable donations went directly to traditional charities and only 6 percent went to private foundations and DAFs. In 2022, the percentage of donations going to traditional charities shrunk considerably, to 59 percent of all donations, with 41 percent instead going private foundations and donor-advised funds—organizations that provide current tax benefits to donors but no assurances the funds will actually be made available for charitable use.

Why, though, would someone set money aside in a private foundation or DAF and not spend it? One reason is because obtaining tax benefits is easy, but charitable giving is hard, particularly for people who aspire to do "very important things." Warren Buffett himself had some insights on this. As he wrote in 2021: "The easiest deed in the world is to give away money that will never be of any real use to you or your family. The giving is painless and may well lead to a better life for both you and your children."[48] The trouble, Buffett suggests, is where the giving has to do more than just provide tax benefits: "The second step of disbursing huge sums is more challenging, particularly when the goal is to focus on crucial problems that have long been difficult to conquer or even dent."[49]

Oracle's CEO Larry Ellison, an original signatory of the Giving Pledge, knows Buffett's pain. Ellison has had public, ongoing difficulty in figuring out how to spend his charitable money—reportedly lurching from project to project, opening one foundation and closing another, spending hundreds of millions of dollars to pursue one goal and abruptly switching to another, with many nonprofits expressing feelings of being abandoned in the process.[50] In the midst of such start-and-stop spending, Ellison's private wealth has continued to grow, from $40 billion at the time of signing the pledge to $192 billion in 2024.

Difficulties in spending money can also prompt many big philanthropists to punt the decision down the road to the next generation. Many do so out of a sincere desire to pass on a culture of philanthropy to their children. But their punt provides a side benefit as well. For those interested in passing power, prestige, and elite connections on to their kids, a well-funded private foundation or donor-advised fund is just the ticket. The ability to make large charitable donations can give their heirs (and *their* heirs) legacy admissions, special treatment in hospitals, and other perks of elite connections, all because the law allows unlimited deferred decision-making.[51]

Buffett has also elected the wealthy parent's model of punting decision-making down the road. After many years of funding the Gates Foundation, Buffett shifted his plan away from the Gateses, and instead, his stated intention is to eventually pass his Berkshire Hathaway stock to a ten-year spend-down private foundation to be controlled by his children, with all spending decisions requiring unanimous consent.[52] This is an interesting strategy. If Buffett's goal is to get his wealth to organizations that can use it, requiring unanimity among siblings would strike most people as a counterproductive system. As Buffett's fellow billionaire-philanthropist John Arnold quipped on the social media platform X: "Warren Buffett is leaving his $127 billion estate to a new charitable trust whose donations must be made by unanimous agreement among his 3 kids. Meanwhile, I can't get my 3 kids to agree from which restaurant to DoorDash dinner."[53]

WHAT DO WE GET FOR OUR INVESTMENT
IN CHARITABLE GIVING? SOMETIMES
MORE THAN WE BARGAIN FOR

Donor-advised funds and private foundations can cause problems for charities because they allow donors to retain control over charitable funds, with no time frame for those funds to ever make their way to charitable ends. As problematic as these bottlenecks can be, sometimes charitable spending can cause even more harms.

That may be hard for some to believe. Like Bernard Marcus said, "What type of numbskull would find something wrong" with money going to charity to help people? But this question is the wrong one, because when we talk about giving by the wealthy, we are rarely talking about traditional charitable giving. Wealthy philanthropists tend to shy away from traditional charity, because they see it as a "mere Band-Aid" or, according to one of the country's first philanthropists, Andrew Carnegie, potentially even worse: "One of the serious obstacles to the improvement of our race is indiscriminate charity. It were better for mankind that the millions of the rich were thrown into the sea than so spent as to encourage the slothful, the drunken, the unworthy. Of every thousand dollars spent in so called charity today, it is probable that $950 is unwisely spent; so spent, indeed, as to produce the very evils which it proposes to mitigate or cure."[54]

Rather, philanthropy is about doing something much grander than mere charity—it's getting to the root source

of the problem. That is why people in philanthropy cir-
cles love to talk about the allegory of the baby in the river,
which goes like this:

> One summer in the village, the people gathered for a picnic.
> As they shared food and conversation, someone noticed a
> baby in the river, struggling and crying. The baby was going
> to drown!
>
> Someone rushed to save the baby. Then, they noticed
> another screaming baby in the river, and they pulled that
> baby out. Soon, more babies were seen drowning in the
> river, and the townspeople were pulling them out as fast as
> they could. It took great effort, and they began to organize
> their activities in order to save the babies as they came down
> the river. As everyone else was busy in the rescue efforts to
> save the babies, two of the townspeople started to run away
> along the shore of the river.
>
> "Where are you going?" shouted one of the rescuers.
> "We need you here to help us save these babies!"
>
> "We are going upstream to stop whoever is throwing
> them in!"[55]

Philanthropists have long seen themselves as the ones
who are best able to find and solve the root causes of problems. Rather than supporters or contributors of existing
charitable endeavors, wealthy philanthropists often choose
to take their own paths. In the words of the sociologist of
wealth Paul Schervish, "They are *producers* rather than supporters of philanthropy."[56] For the wealthiest philanthropists,
this is driven by their own sense of *hyperagency*, their ability

to not just act within rules and resources that are socially given but also to be "a creator or producer of those rules and resources."[57] In *Philanthrocapitalism*, Matthew Bishop and Michael Green tout the value of hyperagency, how it allows wealthy donors to dispense interventions quickly, unilaterally, and without regard for cost or other stakeholders; it "frees them to think long-term, to go against conventional wisdom, to take up ideas too risky for government, to deploy substantial resources quickly when the situation demands it—above all, to try something new."[58]

This approach to philanthropy has achieved some notable successes, changing society for the better in areas or ways that business or government would have otherwise wholly neglected. Julius Rosenwald, the cofounder of Sears, observed that government across the US South refused to invest state money into schools and teachers for Black students, and so he used his vast fortune to build 4,977 schools in Southern locales with significant Black populations. In 1932, the year of his death, 35 percent of all Black children in the South had been educated in one of the Rosenwald schools, which were found to have a profound impact on the equalization of education for Black and white students in the South. Similarly seeking to equalize educational access, the nineteenth-century industrialist Andrew Carnegie paid for 1,795 new libraries to be opened in communities large and small across America. Bill and Melinda Gates also contributed billions to improve health in Africa by working to alleviate or eliminate deadly diseases such as polio, HIV/AIDS, malaria, and tuberculosis.

At the same time, philanthropy is not always an unal-loyed good, and more is not always better. Sometimes phil-anthropic dollars are spent on things that are more in the donor's private interest than in society's larger interest, like promoting disinformation about climate change and fight-ing to reduce taxes for wealthy.

Also, just because someone has money—and maybe even created a successful business—it does not mean that person knows how to solve the problems of the world. Well-meaning people can get in over their head and cre-ate a situation that leaves the beneficiaries worse off than when they started. A good example is Brad Pitt's effort to replace housing destroyed in New Orleans's Ninth Ward by Hurricane Katrina. Pitt created the Make It Right Foun-dation, which crafted a plan to build 109 new sustainable flood-proof affordable houses, all designed by famous ar-chitects and to be sold to the residents of the Ninth Ward at below-market prices. After the houses were built and sold, it turned out that the architects didn't know how to account for the extreme humidity of the region. As a result, the houses were plagued by mold, electrical fires, and un-clean water; the people who bought the houses were left worse off than when they began, still with no place to live, and with all their savings sunk into unlivable houses.[59]

Even experienced philanthropists like Bill and Melinda Gates can make some pretty big mistakes. The Gates Foun-dation has spent billions of dollars promoting various ways to improve education, including replacing large schools with small schools, promoting Common Core learning standards, and evaluating teacher effectiveness through students' test scores. To bring these ideas to fruition, the Gateses not only spent their own charitable funds (already subsidized by taxpayers) but also managed to draw on billions of dollars of federal, state, and local funds to further their initiatives. And yet, there is widespread consensus—including by Gates himself—that none of these efforts produced their desired results.[60]

These mistakes of recent history pale in comparison to the one made by many of the country's most revered philanthropists and their foundations, including Carnegie, Rockefeller, and Russell Sage, as they sought to go upriver to address the sources of society's most pressing problems.

In the late nineteenth century, Sir Francis Galton, a cousin of Charles Darwin, developed a theory that talent and high social rank were hereditary, and that "bountiful breeding of the best people would evolve mankind into a superlative species of grace and quality."[61] Galton himself admitted in 1892 that his theories were completely unprovable, but that did not stop his theory of eugenics from spreading, particularly to America, where suspicions against racial and ethnic groups provided a welcoming environment for the theories of eugenics to take hold.[62]

Still, the theory of eugenics might have remained just a theory but for the fact that the first American foundations became deeply immersed in the effort to promote the reproduction of the "fit" and suppress the reproduction of the "unfit." One of the most significant efforts was by the Carnegie Institution, which funded the creation of a center that worked to find scientific proof to support the eugenics mission.[63] In their zeal, the country's earliest foundations devoted resources not only to research but also to lobbying the government to adopt eugenicist policies. At the federal level, this meant restricting immigration of the "unfit," and at the state level, through mandatory institutionalization and sterilization.

As the historian Edwin Black explains in his exhaustive treatise on the history of the eugenics movement, *War Against the Weak*, the extraordinary amount of philanthropic support appeared to legitimate eugenics, which allowed it to enter popular culture, higher education, and ultimately the legal system, influencing thirty states to pass mandatory sterilization laws and the Supreme Court to uphold them, and persuading Congress to pass a severely restrictive immigration law in 1924 limiting the migration of "defective protoplasm" from Eastern Europe.[64]

The American eugenics movement was not limited to American shores. The movement spread to Germany as well, where it caught the fascination of Adolf Hitler and the Nazi movement, and eventually gave rise to the Final Solution. Because of eugenics' association with Nazi Germany, most states had repealed their eugenics statutes by the end of World War II—but it wasn't until 2020 that the Carnegie Corporation issued a public apology for its support of eugenics.[65]

Hyperagency is not all it's cracked up to be. While government has its own limitations—it can be slow, bureaucratic, and hampered by the need to account for lots of stakeholders—these traits also make it less likely to go one hundred miles an hour down perilous pathways. And while government can no doubt make its own mistakes in backing the wrong horse, it is at least grounded in principles of democracy. We accept the mistakes of the system because it is a system of our own making. This is very different from accepting the mistakes of a rich person making use of our money.

None of this is to say that the tax code should not continue to encourage philanthropy and charitable giving. However, there is no reason to give carte blanche to the richest Americans so they can eliminate their tax liability through charitable giving, particularly when working Americans are limited in their ability to offset their tax liabilities. The wealthiest Americans simply hold too many resources to allow them to abandon the costs of government for the uncertain benefit of their philanthropy. Warren Buffett may believe that he can do better for the world by committing his extraordinary wealth to philanthropy rather than contributing to paying down the national debt, but that doesn't mean we have to agree with him.

6 OUR COMMON WEALTH

When Warren Buffett's secretary Debbie Bosanek returned to Omaha after attending the State of the Union address, she described her experience as being "like a dream come true," one that "she wished everyone could experience."[1] Bosanek understood that her newfound fame and special treatment was due not to something unique about her, but instead to her role as Everyman, a powerful embodiment of an unfair system in which a secretary would be subject to a higher tax burden than her billionaire boss.

Although the Buffett Rule was never adopted, the story of Buffett and his secretary has lived on in the minds of Americans. It is not surprising that this is the case. For over one hundred years, the country has operated under a system that was explicitly designed to impose its greatest burdens on those with the greatest capacity to pay, and it is natural for people to believe that the combination of the income tax imposed at progressive rates and the additional estate tax imposed on the richest 1 percent of Americans is accomplishing that result. While some may cheat, it is not the system that looks to be at fault.

However, as Warren Buffett himself intimated—and as a ProPublica exposé based on the leaked tax returns of the rich confirmed—the tax lives of the rich in the twenty-first century are very different from what the rules appear to provide.[2] While the progressive income tax and the estate tax remain on the books, they no longer accomplish what they were designed to do or what they once did. Today, the system accomplishes the opposite. For those with wealth—like the French aristocracy of yore—taxes are someone else's problem.

While taxes on the richest Americans have become largely elective, the country has accrued a crushing national debt that threatens its ability to meet its most basic expenses. Even more troubling than the fiscal implications is the fact that the country has become a land of two people rather than one: overburdened workers at all income levels carrying the lion's share of the costs of running the country and a growing American aristocracy of wealth and power who are allowed to abdicate their responsibilities to the nation.

This tale of two tax systems has a corrosive effect on society. Describing a similar system in prerevolutionary France, Tocqueville noted that "of all the methods that have been devised for the division of nations into classes, unequal taxes are the most pernicious and effective. They tend to isolate each class irremediably; for when the tax is unequal, the line is drawn afresh every year between the taxables and the exempts; the distinction is never allowed to fade." He added, "Every member of the privileged class feels a pressing and immediate interest in keeping it up, and maintaining his isolation from the taxable community."[3]

For wealthy Americans—like the French aristocracy in Tocqueville's account—maintaining the current system means maintaining a tax code rife with permissive loopholes. Addressing the problem, especially as the country's wealthiest 1 percent own more than 30 percent of the country's wealth, must likewise be centered on the tax code.

The natural answer would seem to be to reinvigorate the estate tax, the one tax specifically aimed at the richest Americans. However, judging by the recent past, this seems exceedingly unlikely to occur: Congress has not closed a single loophole in the estate tax since 1990, even as the tax has become ever more hollowed out by a growing panoply of tax-avoidance techniques.

One reason for this failure to act is the effectiveness of the public relations campaign, which began in the 1990s, to destroy the legitimacy of the estate tax. This campaign effectively transformed the public perception of the tax, from an innocuous backstop to the income tax that added progressivity to the tax system, into an immoral double tax imposed on people at the moment of greatest vulnerability—death.

But history shows that there are other factors, not just effective public relations, that make it unlikely that imposing extra taxes specifically geared to the richest Americans (including the estate tax, or more recent proposals for a wealth tax) will be adopted today.

As this book recounts, the most consequential tax reforms in the history of the United States have occurred when the country's economic system was under threat—specifically, the threat of socialism and communism and their appeals to the working class. For much of the twentieth century, these threats played a critical role in the adoption and expansion of special taxes applied to the very wealthy, imposed as a way of promoting legitimacy for the capitalist order.[4] With the disappearance of socialism and communism from the twenty-first-century political landscape, such threats against capitalism have largely disappeared, which makes special taxes on the rich appear less urgent. Tony Judt, in *Ill Fares the Land*, suggests that the collapse of communism in the 1980s made it easier to stop imposing heavy taxes on the rich, because capitalism was no longer under threat. Moreover, it seems unlikely that these threats will return, given the hegemony of capitalism as a world order, a dynamic described by the economist Branko Milanovic in *Capitalism, Alone*.

Another factor that has tempered the possibility of an updated tax system is the changing nature of war, especially the shift from mass conscription to an all-volunteer professional military. The original estate tax was adopted and expanded amid US involvement in World Wars I and II, during decades when the American working class sacrificed life and livelihood to secure the political fate of the country. The adoption and expansion of an estate tax was one way the country showed its public some measure of reciprocity. This connection is consistent with the research of Kenneth Scheve and David Stasavage, who showed that countries have been most likely to impose taxes on the rich at times of war as a way for the rich to be subject to conscriptions of wealth while the rest of the country was subject to conscriptions of men. As a result, Scheve and Stasavage suggest that as countries like the United States have moved away from mass conscriptions toward a professional volunteer army, they are far less likely to feel the need to impose taxes specifically geared to the rich.

More broadly, the face of wealth in the twenty-first century is different, and differently perceived, than it used to be. At the height of the Gilded Age, the superrich lived in a way that was wholly alien to the average American worker, who peered into opulent New York ballrooms in the same way that we may gaze into a zoo enclosure today.[5] Progressive leaders accused these robber barons and their families of attempting to make a new class of American aristocrats, warning that their newly forming band of economic royalty was dangerous for the nation.[6] The superrich fed the public's accusations of royal aspirations with their homes and ballrooms modeled after foreign palaces; their exhibition of grandiose tiaras and diamond-encrusted dresses; and their armies of servants dressed in the livery of European aristocracy.[7]

Unlike their Gilded Age forebearers, the modern superrich have increasingly shied away from exhibiting their riches as a measure of status. In fact, they now appear to conspicuously avoid it.[8] As the top hats and tiaras of a century ago have been replaced with tennis shoes and quarter-zips, the visible trappings of wealth have merged with those of the middle class; the wealthy and the not wealthy today dress like each other. As the owner of one high-end New York City tailor reported, "When the wealthiest customers walk through the door, more often than not they are wearing old chinos and Sperrys."[9] Warren Buffett, with his lunches at McDonald's and famously frayed ties (prompting Obama to give him a new one to wear during his White House visit), embodies an older version of this look. Elon Musk has publicly embraced a more youthful "everyman" style of T-shirts under blazers, an affectation he famously burnished while smoking cannabis live on the podcast *The Joe Rogan Experience*, attracting worldwide media attention.[10]

Of course, many wealthy continue to engage in behavior that meets the old definitions of conspicuous consumption, flying private jets to kids' soccer practices and living in mansions that would put even the Vanderbilt estate to shame.[11] However, unlike the palaces on Fifth Avenue, these megamansions are increasingly sequestered from the rest of America, in neighborhoods and entire communities segregated by economics.[12] The days of peering through the glass walls of palatial estates to watch diamond-studded debutantes are gone, replaced by the gatehouses of private communities and the brandless athleisure uniforms that disguise their inhabitants.

It is not just the appearances of the wealthy that have changed over the course of the past century. Things have changed for the middle class as well. As the historian John McGerr explains, the post–World War II era was a time of rising wages and a highly egalitarian wage structure (sometimes referred to as *the Great Compression*), buttressed by expansive social programs, new lending programs, and the development of cheap housing for returning American GIs.[13] This created a situation in which regular working Americans could afford to enjoy a version of the lifestyle that had once been the sole purview of the rich: home ownership, college educations, automobiles, and vacations. The golden age of relative income equality produced a golden age of relative cultural equality.[14]

However, since the end of the twentieth century, middle-class Americans have been finding it increasingly difficult to obtain what were once viewed as middle-class staples with their earnings alone.[15] Homeownership, in particular, has become a fundamentally important form of wealth creation for middle-class families, meaning that rising housing prices, especially in urban centers, has hamstrung an entire new generation of prospective middle-class Americans who are unable to buy a home.[16] With the margins tightening, research shows that many Americans now believe that inheritance is one of the only viable ways to achieve the quality of life enjoyed by their forebearers.[17]

As inheritance has become seen as a prerequisite to living the middle-class dream, many middle-class Americans have bought into the idea that limits on inheritances (including the existence of an estate tax) are a threat to their economic security. This is a massive victory for the public relations apparatus that recast the estate tax as a predatory "death tax" affecting everyone, but it also represents a fundamental misunderstanding of the current nature of the estate tax. A poll conducted in 2017 found that 63 percent of respondents believed that the estate tax predominantly affected poor and middle-class families—a belief far from the reality, as more than 99 percent of such estates are untaxed by the federal government.[18]

All this suggests that special taxes specifically geared to the wealthy—like estate taxes or wealth taxes—are less likely to be embraced by the American public than one might expect. But there is another way forward to bring the country together to share the costs of our democracy, and that is to reform the broad-based income tax to bring in the most common sources of wealth for America's ultra-wealthy: their investments and inheritances.

A precursor to doing so would be to introduce honesty into the debate about who carries the costs of government. Across countries and throughout history, the wealthiest people have always sought to avoid taxes to preserve their wealth and power. The French aristocracy did so directly, through explicit rules that excluded them from the reach of taxes. However, this type of explicit exclusion is unlikely to work in a democracy based on principles of equality where preferential tax avenues for the rich must be hidden from public view. This is the case in the United States.

By concealing their highly lucrative paths to tax avoidance, wealthy people have succeeded in maintaining secrecy about what their actual tax liabilities are. If one wished to find out how much tax those with high wealth (as opposed to those with high income) pay—or don't pay—the information would be surprisingly difficult to find. One reason is because the most accurate source of information about how much people pay—actual tax returns—are protected from public scrutiny by strict privacy laws. This stands in sharp contrast to a brief period in the early part of the twentieth century, when the richest individuals and corporations had their names and tax liabilities published on the front page of *The New York Times*.[19]

This modern secrecy was at least partially lifted in 2022, when the IRS employee Charles Littlejohn leaked data to journalists, giving them access to a vast cache of tax returns of the richest Americans. The series of ProPublica stories that followed revealed how many of America's wealthiest citizens—including Michael Bloomberg, Jeff Bezos, George Soros, and Elon Musk—paid little or nothing in taxes.[20] While these stories should have been enough to shift people's understanding about who does and does not pay taxes, the response to the ProPublica leak was muted by a barrage of articles about the propriety of ProPublica's actions in publishing the tax information and by statistics around income taxes paid by those with high incomes. These responses, which inaccurately conflated the tax burdens of those with high incomes and those with great wealth, sought to portray the ProPublica stories as deviations from some larger norm in which the rich were doing their part.

These occasional, brief glimpses into the tax lives of the rich are exceptions to the larger rule that the tax world inhabited by the wealthy is a secret one, and the vast inequities of it are unexamined. But illustrations of their principles can be still seen in the wild.

Consider the case of a person with a $1 million salary (subject to roughly $370,000 in income taxes) who also receives a $100 million inheritance. Under current reporting rules, only the $1 million salary is reported, giving the impression—to the taxpayer, the IRS, and the public at large—that the taxpayer with $1 million in income will pay taxes at a rate of 37 percent. Were the taxpayer required to report the $100 million inheritance as well, it would be easy to see that the actual total tax burden would be less than 1 percent of the income acquired in that year.

These reporting systems are also puzzlingly scatter-shot. Whereas the receipt of the inheritance in our example does not require reporting, other types of income, even income not subject to tax, does require reporting. Income from tax-exempt bonds, distributions from Roth IRAs, and capital gains on the sale of a house must all be reported on taxpayers' annual tax returns, even though they are not subject to tax. The reporting is a good thing: It gives policy makers the ability to determine the cost to the federal government of excluding these items from taxation. But it also makes the institutionalized failure to require such reporting for gifts and inheritances all the more disturbing.

The lack of good public information about how much tax the wealthy pay has facilitated the proliferation of false and misleading statistics. The most powerful and often-cited statistic states that the top 1 percent of income earners pay almost 40 percent of all income taxes, while the bottom 40 percent of earners pay no income taxes at all.[21] Such statistical accounts are often used in misleading ways by conflating high earners with high wealth owners. While it is true that these high-income earners do indeed pay the most income taxes, it says nothing about the wealthiest Americans, who—because of their ability to avoid taxable income, particularly for their investments and inheritances—are just as likely to be in the bottom 40 percent of income earners who pay no taxes as they are in the top 1 percent.

The lack of real information about who pays how much in taxes, together with the various myths that support the current regime, combine to support the notion that our system is working for the good of all, when in fact, it allows the wealthiest to opt out entirely.

A final source of misinformation has been public communication about the nature of payroll taxes. The failure to describe payroll taxes as real taxes may have been valuable in terms of securing the political viability of the Social Security system in its early days, and no doubt makes it more resistant to political change, but it has also served to distort the public's perception about who pays the costs of running the country's most expensive programs, its social insurance programs. We are no longer living in the days of Coxey's Army when the vulnerabilities of old-age disability and unemployment were seen as something that we should all manage for ourselves. Instead, the protections provided by Social Security and Medicare are essential features of a modern economy, and workers should be recognized for the costs they carry in providing them.

An intellectually honest, public discussion of what the tax system does for wealthy people would be a victory in itself. Making progress beyond that would require a set of solutions to reverse the damage that has been done and to recalibrate the US tax system as something other than an apparatus for consolidating wealth. However, this goal is not beyond reach. The path to doing so involves three steps: (1) repealing the estate tax, (2) bringing inheritances and investments into the income tax system, and (3) reforming the rules around philanthropy to strengthen the charitable sector, while ensuring that everyone plays a role in supporting the country's expenses.

REPEAL THE ESTATE TAX

The first step toward ensuring that the wealthy support the costs of government is to repeal the estate tax.

The estate tax was enacted for two important reasons: to generate revenue and curtail large inheritances of wealth, the latter of which were seen as a threat to democracy. However, whatever the estate tax might have achieved in the past, it clearly no longer does so. The revenue it now raises (only $30 billion in 2024, less than 0.5 percent of the country's total revenue) is minuscule, an amount so small that Elon Musk could gain or lose it over the course of a day and not notice the difference. And the continuing power of large inheritances to persist through generations is seen in the annual Forbes 400 list, on which a full 30 percent of those listed appear simply due to luck of birth. The effect of billionaires' wealth on our democracy was more evident than ever in the presidential election of 2024, in which support for Joe Biden and Donald Trump was largely characterized in terms of which billionaires supported which candidate. In the highly polarized United States, politics today has the appearances of "our" billionaires versus "theirs."

Meanwhile, as the estate tax accomplishes none of its goals, its continued existence produces affirmative harms, principal among which is its sowing of a distorted public understanding about the actual tax burden borne by the wealthiest Americans. Unlike with payroll taxes, which are largely hidden from public view but disproportionally burden those at the other end of the wealth distribution, the estate tax has been front and center for an American public that has been made hyperaware of it from the antitax campaign that began in the late 1990s and continues today. The effect of this hyperawareness of the estate tax is to provide a protective shield for the rich, making the public believe that rich Americans pay not just one set of taxes, but two.

Harms caused by the estate tax go far beyond providing public relations cover for the rich; its continued existence imposes financial costs as well. That is because the income tax system has been developed on the basis of the assumption of the existence of a robust estate tax. Because of that assumption, the income tax has conspicuously avoided the most common sources of wealth of the richest Americans: inheritances and investments. In other words, the existence of the estate tax has served to legitimate the shortcomings of the income tax system.

The effect of excluding gifts and inheritances from the income tax is that these sources of income are not only not taxed to the recipient—they are not even reported (nor are the costs of the exclusion calculated in the tax expenditure budget). This exclusion from income taxes is understandable in a world where there is a robust estate and gift tax imposing heavy taxes on these transfers for the giver. However, without a meaningful estate tax, the exclusion is nonsensical. When a lucky heir receives a windfall inheritance or gift, that is just as much income as are earnings, lottery winnings, prize money, or found money on the street—all of which are subject to income taxes at the highest ordinary income rates. A system that requires someone who earns $100,000 to pay almost 30 percent in payroll and income taxes while giving another person who inherits $10 million a free pass is indefensible—which is why the system relies so heavily on misinformation.

Although the tax code does not explicitly exclude investment gains from the income tax, the results are the same as if it did. Through techniques like buy, borrow, die, which allows owners of wealth to defer taxes on gains until they are sold and, accordingly, to avoid taxes altogether by holding investments until death—the evasion of income taxes is institutionalized. And this is allowed to persist because of an assumption of a functioning estate tax.

BRING INHERITANCES AND INVESTMENTS
INTO THE INCOME TAX SYSTEM

The income tax plays an important role in American life. Of all the taxes, it regularly provides the most revenue to the country, and in 2024, the amount that it raised—$2.43 trillion—constituted almost half of all government revenue. Because of the requirement to file annual tax returns, income tax is the tax with which Americans are most familiar. And tellingly, because of the country's heavy dependence on the income tax system, it is one of the few taxes that gets regular attention from Congress.

Given the preeminence and centrality of the income tax system, it seems odd to not have it apply to the sources of income most common for the richest Americans: inheritances and investments. Two simple reforms can solve this problem: Tax the receipt of inheritances and gifts under the income tax system (allowing for certain transfers to occur tax-free), and tax unrealized gains at death on the final income tax return of the decedent.

Repeal the Exclusion for Inheritances and Gifts

Objectively, money received as gifts and inheritances fits within the parameters of the income tax, which applies broadly (to quote the tax code) to "all income from whatever source derived."[22] The reason it is not subject to tax, however, is that a different section of the code says that "gross income does not include the value of property acquired by gift, bequest, devise, or inheritance."[23] By repealing this exclusion (in conjunction with repealing the estate tax), the entire tax code would be fairer while also bringing the wealthy into the purview of the same tax system that applies to the vast majority of Americans.

The proposal to tax inheritances under the income tax system (as opposed to the ineffectual estate tax system) has been proposed by a number of scholars over the years, most recently by former Assistant Treasury Secretary Lily Batchelder.[24] There are several reasons it would be a preferable way to tax inheritances instead of through the estate tax system.

First, taxing inheritances as income fits in with people's basic understanding of the income tax. Through filing annual tax returns, many Americans have become familiar with the expansive definition of income, and the inclusion of large inheritances and gifts is very much in keeping with a system that already taxes not just earnings and other rent but also lottery winnings, prize money, and found money on the street. The exclusion of gifts and inheritances is an anomaly to this comprehensive system and one that many people don't even know exists. Indeed, as others have noted, and I myself have experienced, many people mistakenly assume that large gifts and inheritances are already subject to income tax.[25]

Second, taxing inheritances to heirs rather than estates gets away from the perception that the estate tax is an unfair double tax imposed on dead people. Both estate taxes and inheritance taxes are borne financially by the recipient of the property, who receives that property only after taxes have been paid. However, by imposing the tax on the decedent's estate, the estate tax is susceptible to being perceived as a tax on the dead person, perhaps on wealth that was already subject to the income tax system.[26]

By contrast, taxes imposed on heirs upon the receipt of property are far less vulnerable to such charges. The recipient of an inheritance is receiving a windfall, and given the breadth of the income tax, it is entirely in keeping that it should be subject to tax. In addition, by taxing the recipient rather than the estate, the tax is much fairer because the rate can align with the economic status of each recipient, so that someone who has more overall income from all sources (including inheritances) is taxed at a higher overall rate than someone who has less. This is unlike the estate tax, for which the tax rate is set based on the size of the estate of the transferor.

Some are under the mistaken assumption that if the decedent paid income taxes when acquiring the property, then it would be an unfair double tax for the heir to do so as well. But there is no such principle in tax law. If a car owner pays taxes on money earned at her job, and then pays a mechanic to fix her car, the mechanic cannot avoid income taxes on that money received because it was previously taxed as income to the car owner.

To accommodate parents' common desire to provide basic support for their children, and to allow for people to support each other without government interference, the income tax on gifts and inheritances could provide the same exclusions that are currently available for gift tax purposes; these allow for property to pass tax-free to spouses and also for people to provide educational and medical expenses, as well as $18,000 per year to anyone else, tax-free. In addition, the rule could allow each person to inherit up to $1 million and pay income taxes only on anything in excess of that.

As for family businesses, the rules could provide an exception for family farms and businesses of moderate size (perhaps subject to a $20 million cap) for those heirs actively involved in the business. But any such exception must be mindful that what works well for moderate estates would be harmful if allowed for large ones. There is no reason we should promote the creation of dynastic wealth by giving a free pass on taxes as multibillion-dollar businesses—like Walmart, Koch Industries, and Mars—get passed from generation to generation, particularly because the way that wealth passed this way magnifies political power. As the tax scholar James Repetti has written: "It is one thing to deal with a more powerful person than yourself; it is another to consider that your children will have to deal with the children of the powerful person, and that your grandchildren will have to deal with her grandchildren. . . . In its worst form, of course, this creates a royalty, a concern addressed in a famous quote attributed to Alexis de Tocqueville: 'What is most important for democracy is not that great fortunes should not exist, but that great fortunes should not remain in the same hands.'"[27]

Our experience with families with dynastic wealth undermining the estate tax provides good evidence of the problems dynastic wealth can create.

Look North; or, Tax Unrealized Gains at Death

As has been discussed, there are many practical reasons for not taxing unrealized gains during life, most notably due to the difficulty of valuation and also problems raised by potential lack of liquidity, if people have to pay tax on unrealized gains. However, while these justifications make a lot of sense during a person's life, they no longer do once that person has given up ownership. Both President Nixon and President Obama proposed that, to create a fairer tax system that treats investment income more like income from earnings, gains should be taxed upon the transfer of property by gift or at death. This rule was adopted in Canada, and we should do so here to ensure that those gains are taxed to the person who earned them.[28]

Just looking at the Forbes 400 list, there are hundreds of billions, and perhaps even trillions, of dollars in untaxed gains. Recent research from the Brookings Institution suggests that as much as one-third of all bequeathable wealth comprises unrealized gains.[29] There is no reason for the American tax system to give owners of those profits a free pass. In addition, taxing gains when property is transferred by gift or at death solves many problems of our current rules, most importantly, the problem of lock-in effect, which has a distortionary effect on markets. If owners knew their gains were certain to be taxed, they would base their decisions about whether to sell or hold on perceptions of the asset's market value rather than the opportunities for tax avoidance.[30]

REFORM PHILANTHROPY

Tax rules governing philanthropy are also in need of reform. Charities play an essential role in American society, and we need to make sure that they have the resources they need to do their work. At the same time, the government needs to have the resources it needs to do its work. The rules of philanthropy should be reformed to accomplish both goals.

This is not the first time this work has been done. The 1969 rules—treating public charities differently from private foundations—put a comprehensive system in place designed to ensure that charitable dollars made their way to charitable ends within a reasonable period. But the rise of donor-advised funds has made it easy to evade those rules.

To address this, Congress should impose meaningful payout rules on donor-advised fund accounts (not on sponsors who can easily game the rules) and private foundations to make clear that contributions to donor-controlled intermediaries are not the same as outright donations to working charities.

Finally, and most importantly, Congress should impose limits on charitable tax benefits for capital gains and estate and gift tax purposes that are similar to those imposed in the income tax world. For example, if Warren Buffett transfers $100 billion to his kids' private foundation, the charitable deduction could be limited to 50 percent, ensuring that at least some of his wealth is subject to tax so it can be used to meet some of the expenses of government, like paying down the national debt. In this way, wealthy donors will still be able to commit their funds for the public good while a portion of their money goes to sharing the costs of government.

THE NEED FOR REFORM, NOT JUST MONEY

After Tocqueville wrote *Democracy in America* to great international acclaim, he returned to his family home in Normandy to study his own country to gain a better understanding about what had happened to cause the French Revolution. In the end, he determined that the critical factor was taxes. Not just because of the financial burdens they imposed on the poor, or the way they undermine adequate revenue for the country, but for the larger effect that the disparate treatment of the rich had on society as a whole, creating divisions that permeated all aspects of life. As he wrote: "All, or nearly all public measures begin or end with a tax. Hence, when two classes of citizens do not feel the taxes alike, they cease to have common interests and feelings in common; they do not require to meet for consultation; they have no opportunity and no desire to act in concert."[31]

Unlike prerevolutionary France, the United States was founded on principles of equality. These principles, though incomplete at conception, have served as a continuing guide for the ongoing process of building "a more perfect union." Bringing the rich back into the tax system is an essential step in this ongoing endeavor.

Acknowledgments

A book like this has many authors. This is especially true here, where my goal has been a challenging one: to find a way to engage the public in a topic many people are inclined to find intimidating, boring, or both. To the extent I have succeeded, it is in great part due to the efforts and insights of the people listed here who generously offered their time, attention, wisdom, and willingness to engage in the intricacies of the tax code—perhaps more than they would have liked—but always with intelligence, good humor, and kindness.

My most profound gratitude goes to my editor Chad Zimmerman, truly without whom this book would not exist. Chad had an unwavering vision of this book's possibilities that served as a North Star for me throughout the whole writing process. Writing a book can be a lonely affair, yet Chad was there the whole way through—far beyond what any author has a right to expect—offering support, encouragement, wisdom, and, when needed, hard truths. Through it all he was not just an extraordinary editor but has become one of my favorite people as well.

And I am so grateful to Sam Stoloff, my extraordinary agent, for his willingness to be inspired by the "Tax the Rich" pin of Frances Goldin to take on a book on tax policy and set it on its right path.

I also owe a special debt of gratitude to Michael Ryan, who set me straight when I wavered on my path, and who, along with Lili Lynton, provided incredibly helpful feedback at all stages of this project.

I am grateful to the people at Boston College Law School, my academic home for over three decades. First and foremost, to my extraordinary students whose fresh perspectives—and outrage—about our tax system have inspired me to do this work. I am also tremendously grateful to my colleagues and friends at the law school, with special appreciation to Bill Bagley, Sergio Campos, Aziz Rana, Jim Repetti, and Steve Shay for reading the complete manuscript and offering helpful suggestions, and a special debt of gratitude to Alicia Munnell, founder of the Center for Retirement Research at Boston College, for her expert input on matters of Social Security. I also want to thank my colleagues Roger Colinvaux and Brian Galle for freely sharing their expertise in matters of tax policy and philanthropy.

Karen Breda, along with Amy Bruce, provided everything I could hope for in a librarian. They received my endless questions with good humor, and if there was an answer to be found, they found it. My research assistants Oliver Russell, Reagan McGinnis, Jeff Minjae Kim, and Chris Fitzgerald offered extraordinary help with the research and writing of this book. And Scott Sheltra and Eric Hardy provided not just great administrative support but encouragement as well. Special thanks to Ben Bardeen from dining services who kept daily tabs on the book and its progress.

I owe special thanks to Helen Flannery, who provided powerful data visualization (called dreamy by some) that really brought this information to life, and Chuck Collins—both for his generosity in sharing Helen with me and for his great work leading the charge for a fairer tax system and more equitable world.

I am also grateful to the team at the University of Chicago Press, especially Katherine Faydash for her superb copyediting work, Rosemary Frehe for her work on the images and shepherding the text, and Lindsy Rice for managing all aspects of production. I also want to thank Carrie Olivia Adams and Angela Baggetta for guiding this book through the most critical last leg of any book's journey—to its readers. I am so grateful for your knowledge and guidance.

And to my dream team, my dearest friends and family, who have supported me every step along the way, listening to me talk about taxes and the ups and downs of the writing process on our frequent walks, talks, and texts, reading drafts, and providing important insights that have made their way into these pages: Lorraine Anastasio, Bruce and Annie Aune, Sharon Beckman, my comrade and guide in writing Susan Bell, Heidi Brown, Mike Cassidy, Allison Chernow, Andrew Dreyfus, Jacqueline Fedida, Debra Fine, Jackie Asadorian Fishbein, Gigi Georges, Gary Gulman, Sarah Hemphill, Phil Johnson, my loving and supportive siblings, Emily, Robbie, and Harriet Madoff, Steve Merkel, Eve Minkoff, Julia Nourok, Michael Orey, Harvey Rishikof, Dan Schlesinger, Mary Schneider, Robin Shanus, Dina Temple-Raston, and Charlie Walsh. Your fingerprints are all over this, and I am so grateful for their presence.

Finally, to Dave, Gabe, Jesse, and Milly. What would I be without you? You make my world go around, and I am so grateful for you every day. I dedicate this book to you.

Notes

PREFACE

1. See Gary Gulman's comedy routine at "In This Economy," YouTube video, 6:39, https://www.youtube.com/watch?v=A1hP9M0MNdo.

2. In the years since 1980, the ratio of wealth and the attached inequality have far outpaced the reductive effects of inflation. Edward Wolff, "Why the Middle Class Benefits from Inflation," Centre for Economic Policy Research, January 8, 2024, https://cepr.org/voxeu/columns/why-middle-class-benefits-inflation. See also Dong-Hyeon Kim and Shu-Chin Lin, "Inflation and Wealth Inequality," *Economic Analysis and Policy* 82 (June 2024): 893–907, https://doi.org/10.1016/j.eap.2024.04.016.

3. Chase Peterson-Withorn, "Forbes 400: The Definitive Ranking of America's Richest People 2024," *Forbes*, https://www.forbes.com/forbes-400/.

4. For a recent example, see Jessica Riedl, "Correcting the Top 10 Tax Myths," December 12, 2024, Manhattan Institute, https://manhattan.institute/article/correcting-the-top-10-tax-myths.

5. "Total Net Worth Held by the Top 1% (99th to 100th Wealth Percentiles) Q2, 2024," Federal Reserve Economic Data (FRED), Federal Reserve Bank of St. Louis, https://fred.stlouisfed.org/series/WFRBLT01026. By the end of the year this amount had risen to $49.46 billion. "Total Net Worth Held by the Top 1% (99th to 100th Wealth Percentiles) Q4, 2024," Federal Reserve Economic Data (FRED), Federal Reserve Bank of St. Louis.

CHAPTER ONE

1. Barack Obama, *The Audacity of Hope: Thoughts on Reclaiming the American Dream* (Crown, 2006), 189.

2. Warren E. Buffett, "Stop Coddling the Super-Rich," *New York Times*, August 15, 2011, https://www.nytimes.com/2011/08/15/opinion/stop-coddling-the-super-rich.html.

3. Barack Obama, "Remarks by the President in State of the Union Address," White House, Office of the Press Secretary, January 24, 2012, https://obamawhitehouse.archives.gov/the-press-office/2012/01/24/remarks-president-state-union-address.

4. Kim Geiger, "Polls: Americans Divided Over Taxes but Support 'Buffett Rule,'" *Los Angeles Times*, April 16, 2012, https://www.latimes.com/business/la-xpm-2012-apr-16-la-pn-polls-americans-divided-over-taxes-but-support-buffett-rule-20120416-story.html.

5. According to Buffett's op-ed, his tax liability (presumably for 2010) was 17.4 percent of his income, generating a tax liability of just under $7 million. Doing the math his total taxable income would have been $40 million (since $7 million is 17.4 percent of $40 million). Presumably that income was generated by capital gains and dividends from Buffett's personal investments, outside of Berkshire Hathaway, since Buffett only took a modest salary and Berkshire Hathaway did not distribute profits. If Buffett had been subject to the Buffett Rule that year, his tax rate would have been 30 percent and his bill would have been about $12 million (an increase of $5 million). Although this sounds like a big number—and to the vast majority of Americans it is—$12 million in annual taxes would have had only a negligible impact on Buffett's growing wealth. According to Forbes, from 2010 to 2011, Buffett's wealth grew by $10 billion, so even if Buffett paid the 30 percent tax of $12 million, that would have represented only 0.12 percent of this growth. The $12 million in taxes is even smaller in relation to Buffett's total wealth, which that year was $47 billion, making Buffett's tax payment less than 0.02 percent of his total wealth. Luisa Kroll, "The World's Billionaires," *Forbes*, March 10, 2010 (updated July 11, 2012), https://www.forbes.com/2010/03/10/worlds-richest-people-slim-gates-buffett-billionaires-2010_land.html.

6. With Warren Buffett at the helm, there was only one year in which Berkshire Hathaway issued a dividend: 1967. Buffett later joked that he must have been in the bathroom when the decision was made. Timothy Smith, "Why Doesn't Berkshire Hathaway Pay a Dividend?," Investopedia, August 8, 2023, https://www.investopedia.com/ask/answers/021615/why-doesnt-berkshire-hathaway-pay-dividend.asp.

7. Charles Adams, *For Good and Evil: The Impact of Taxes on the Course of Civilization*, 2nd ed. (Madison Books, 1999), 222.

8. According to IRS data cited at the US Treasury Department's Fiscal-Data website, "From 1868 until 1913, 90% of all federal revenue came from taxes on liquor, beer, wine, and tobacco." "How Much Revenue Has the U.S. Government Collected This Year?," FiscalData.Treasury.gov, 2024, https://fiscaldata.treasury.gov/americas-finance-guide/government-revenue/.

9. Although World War I saw the American trade surplus grow from $541 million in 1914 to $4.4 billion in 1919, the rapid decline in imports saw custom receipts drop by a third after 1914. Michael Levy, "Underwood-Simmons Tariff Act," *Encyclopaedia Britannica*, 2025, https://www.britannica.com/topic/New-Freedom.

10. See generally Ganesh Sitaraman, *The Crisis of the Middle-Class Constitution: Why Economic Inequality Threatens Our Republic* (Vintage Books, 2018).

11. With top estate tax rates reaching as high as 77 percent during the period from 1940 to 1977. "Historical Look at Estate and Gift Tax Rates," Wolters Kluwer, https://www.wolterskluwer.com/en/expert-insights/whole-ball-of-tax-historical-estate-and-gift-tax-rates. When these taxes were first adopted, they applied to only the wealthiest 3 percent of Americans. In the wake of World War II, the income tax was expanded to apply more broadly—it has often been described as going from a class tax to a "mass tax." Another change took place over time as well: When first adopted, the taxes were imposed at relatively modest rates, with income taxes at a top rate of 7 percent and estate taxes at a top rate of 10 percent. However, as the country faced two world wars and weathered the Great Depression, tax rates increased, to a top income tax rate of 90 percent and a top estate tax rate of 77 percent.

12. Graphs showing the amount of wealth owned by the wealthiest Americans have a distinct U-shaped curve. Starting in the early part of the twentieth century, at the height of the Gilded Era, the wealthiest 1 percent owned a little more than one-third of the country's wealth. By the mid-1970s, wealth concentration was at its lowest levels, with the wealthiest Americans owning about 20 percent of the country's wealth, and it began its ascent to today, when the richest Americans again control 30 percent of the country's wealth. See Emmanuel Saez and Gabriel Zucman, *The Triumph on Injustice: How the Rich Dodge Taxes and How to Make Them Pay* (W. W. Norton and Co., 2020), 98.

13. "What Is the National Deficit?," FiscalData.Treasury.gov, https://fiscaldata.treasury.gov/americas-finance-guide/national-deficit/.

14. "What Is the National Debt Costing Us?," Peter G. Peterson Foundation, August 6, 2024, https://www.pgpf.org/blog/2024/08/what-is-the-national-debt-costing-us.

15. Jesse Eisinger, Jeff Ernsthausen, and Paul Kiel, "The Secret IRS Files: Trove of Never-Before-Seen Records Reveal How the Wealthiest Avoid Income Tax," ProPublica, June 8, 2021, https://www.propublica.org/article/the-secret-irs-files-trove-of-never-before-seen-records-reveal-how-the-wealthiest-avoid-income-tax. Charles Littlejohn was later sentenced to five years in prison for his role in illuminating this closely guarded tax information. "Former IRS Contractor Sentenced for Disclosing Tax Return Information to News Organizations," Office of Public Affairs, January 29, 2024, https://www.justice.gov/opa/pr/former-irs-contractor-sentenced-disclosing-tax-return-information-news-organizations.

16. Gigi Zamora, "The 2024 Self-Made Score: From Bootstrappers to Silver Spooners," *Forbes*, October 1, 2024, https://www.forbes.com/sites/gigizamora/2024/10/01/the-2024-forbes-400-self-made-billionaire-score-from-bootstrappers-to-silver-spooners/.

17. Moore v. United States, 602 U.S. 572 (2024).

18. Emmanuel Saez and Gabriel Zucman, "Progressive Wealth Taxation," *Brookings Papers on Economic Activity*, Fall 2019, 437–533, https://www.brookings.edu/articles/progressive-wealth-taxation/.

19. Elon Musk received zero salary in 2020, causing the State of California to complain that Tesla was breaking its minimum-wage laws by not paying him at least $23,000. Chris Isidore, "Elon Musk: Zero Pay but Tens of Billions in Stock Options in 2020," CNN, August 14, 2021, https://www.cnn.com/2021/08/14/business/elon-musk-pay/index.html.

20. From 1954 to 2003, dividends were generally subject to tax at ordinary income tax rates, the same as applied to salaries. In 2003, dividends began to be taxed at a reduced rate of 15 percent.

21. Some of these techniques were discussed in the article by Jesse Drucker, "How One of the World's Richest Men Is Avoiding $8 Billion in Taxes," *New York Times*, December 5, 2024, https://www.nytimes.com/2024/12/05/business/nvidia-jensen-huang-estate-taxes.html.

22. Lisa Keister, "Income and Wealth Are Not Highly Correlated: Here Is Why and What It Means," *Work in Progress*, October 29, 2018, http://www.wipsociology.org/2018/10/29/income-and-wealth-are-not-highly-correlated-here-is-why-and-what-it-means/.

23. Martin Wolfe, *The Crisis of Democratic Capitalism* (Penguin Random House, 2023).

CHAPTER TWO

1. As a highly successful performer, Steve Martin would have been particularly sensitive to taxes in the 1970s when the highest marginal income tax rates were 70 percent. His memoir is *Born Standing Up: A Comic's Life* (Scribner, 2007). The millionaire routine is found on Martin's 1979 stand-up album *Comedy Is Not Pretty!* (Warner Bros.).

2. While income taxes provide for an exemption amount, payroll taxes are collected at the first dollar earned. The Earned Income Tax Credit can reduce or even eliminate the tax burden for some low earners, but the cutoff level is shockingly low. This is particularly so for those taxpayers without children. To be eligible for the credit, a childless adult would need to earn less than $18,591.

3. For a full discussion of the arguments for and against estate taxes, see Walter J. Blum, "A Handy Summary of the Capital Gains Arguments," *Taxes: The Tax Magazine*, April 1957. Although this article lists a number of arguments on both sides of the issue of a preferential rate, there is a general consensus among tax scholars that there are few substantial arguments in favor of the preferential rate. See, e.g., Noel B. Cunningham and Deborah H. Schenk, "The Case for a Capital Gains Preference," *Tax Law Review* 48 (1993): 319–80. "For years, the authors have taught their students that we could identify no substantial argument to support a preference for capital gains in a tax system with Haig-Simons income as the normative tax base. Indeed, the arguments against the preference were so strong that it was hard to construct a competing claim. Although we acknowledged serious flaws in the current treatment of capital gains, we asserted that a preference appeared to be a very poor solution to any of these problems" (320). Upon reexamination, the authors continue: "We found all arguments favoring the preference wanting. Each serious contention reacts to a flaw in the current treatment of capital gains that stems from the realization requirement" (320).

4. Reagan's proposal also included adjustment for inflation for long-term capital gains, but that did not end up in the bill. Floyd Norris, "Tax Reform Might Start with a Look Back to '86," *New York Times*, November 22, 2012, https://www.nytimes.com/2012/11/23/business/a-starting-point-for-tax -reform-what-reagan-did.html.

5. Some blame President Bush's subsequent 1992 loss on this violation of his "read my lips, no new taxes" pledge. Ron Elving, "6 Little Words Helped Make George H. W. Bush (A 1-Term) President," *All Things Considered* (NPR), December 4, 2018, https://www.npr.org/2018/12/04/673249018/6 -little-words-helped-make-george-h-w-bush-a-one-term-president.

6. Andrew W. Mellon, *Taxation: The People's Business* (Macmillan Co., 1924), 56–57.

7. "Topic No. 420, Bartering Income," Internal Revenue Service, June 12, 2024, https://www.irs.gov/taxtopics/tc420.

8. Self-employed individuals bear payroll taxes in the entirety (although only 92.35 percent of the self-employed income is subject to income taxes). For those who are not self-employed, employees pay half the tax, and their employer pays the other half. Even in that situation, though, economists agree that the employer likely passes on the economic burden of its share to the employee in terms of reduced wages.

9. Several tech CEOs have taken low salaries, including Steve Jobs, who took just $1 every year (except for 2001, when Apple gifted its founder a private jet plane). Google founders Larry Page and Sergey Brin also only take $1 a year each. Former Oracle CEO Larry Ellison used to take $1 in salary but was routinely among America's highest-paid CEOs because he took home a ton in stock awards. David Goldman, "Jeff Bezos Made $81,840 Last Year. He's Still the Richest Person in the World," CNN, April 11, 2019, https://www.cnn.com/2019/04/11/tech/jeff-bezos-pay/index.html.

10. Jonathan Goldstein and John Rubinetti, "2021 North American Private Equity Investment Professional Compensation Survey: Insights: Heidrick & Struggles," Heidrick & Struggles, 2021, https://www.heidrick.com/en/insights/private-equity/2021-north-american-private-equity-investment-professional-compensation-survey.

11. Hank Tucker, "As Profits Rise, Private Equity Billionaires Have Huge Paydays," *Forbes*, March 2, 2022, https://www.forbes.com/sites/hanktucker/2022/02/28/as-profits-rise-private-equity-billionaires-have-huge-paydays/.

12. Tania Mitra, "Blackstone CEO Steve Schwarzman Took Home $896M in 2023," Citywire Pro Buyer, February 29, 2024, https://citywire.com/pro-buyer/news/blackstone-ceo-steve-schwarzman-took-home-896m-in-2023/a2437317.

13. Paul Kiel and Mick Dumke, "Why Citadel's Ken Griffin Spent $54 Million to Defeat an Illinois Tax Increase," ProPublica, July 7, 2022, https://www.propublica.org/article/ken-griffin-illinois-graduated-income-tax.

14. Hank Tucker, "The Richest Hedge Fund Managers 2023," *Forbes*, April 6, 2023, https://www.forbes.com/sites/hanktucker/2023/04/04/the-richest-hedge-fund-managers-2023/.

15. Data compiled from Chase Peterson-Withorn, "Forbes 400: The Definitive Ranking of America's Richest People 2024," *Forbes*, 2024, https://www.forbes.com/forbes-400/.

16. A typical compensation structure gives the fund advisers a management fee of 2 percent of the amount of money under management and an

additional 20 percent of the fund's profits over a certain threshold. Under current tax rules, fund managers treat the 2 percent management fee as ordinary income and the 20 percent as capital gains, for their investment of time and expertise. Payment for services—even those payments contingent on profits, like contingent royalties—is a classic example of employment compensation and as such should be taxed at ordinary income rates, but under carried-interest rules, it is treated as capital gains.

17. "Federal Income Tax Rates and Brackets," Internal Revenue Service (for 2023), https://www.irs.gov/filing/federal-income-tax-rates-and-brackets.

18. While Trump promised to "eliminate the carried-interest deduction" on the 2016 campaign trail, his 2017 tax reforms took a more anemic approach. The new rules simply changed the holding period: Under the new rules, investment managers must hold the assets for three years instead of one. However, most private equity funds hold their assets for more than five years, so the longer holding period does not affect them much. Louis Jacobson, "Trump-O-Meter: PolitiFact," PolitiFact, December 20, 2017, https://www.politifact.com/truth-o-meter/promises/trumpometer/promise/1429/eliminate-carried-interest-loophole/; "What Is Carried Interest, and How Is It Taxed?," Tax Policy Center, January 2024, https://www.taxpolicycenter.org/briefing-book/what-carried-interest-and-how-it-taxed.

19. Jennifer Szalai, "Going Bankrupt in the Name of Efficiency," *New York Times*, June 21, 2023, https://www.nytimes.com/2023/06/21/books/review/plunder-brendan-ballou-these-are-the-plunderers-gretchen-morgenson-joshua-rosner.html.

20. Associated Press, "Kyrsten Sinema's Donations from Investors Surged to Nearly $1 Million in the Year Before She Killed a Huge New Tax on Private Equity and Hedge Funds," *Fortune*, August 15, 2022, https://fortune.com/2022/08/13/sinema-wall-street-money-killing-tax-investors/; Brian Schwartz, "How Wall Street Wooed Sen. Kyrsten Sinema and Preserved Its Multibillion-Dollar Carried Interest Tax Break," CNBC, August 10, 2022, https://www.cnbc.com/2022/08/09/how-wall-street-wooed-sen-kyrsten-sinema-and-preserved-its-multi-billion-dollar-carried-interest-tax-break.html.

21. "Baldwin, Manchin, Brown Lead Effort to Close Tax Loophole and Make Private Equity Pay Their Fair Share," US Senator Tammy Baldwin, April 15, 2024, https://www.baldwin.senate.gov/news/press-releases/baldwin-manchin-brown-lead-effort-to-close-tax-loophole-and-make-private-equity-pay-their-fair-share.

22. In March 2023, Uber stock was trading at $31 per share, allowing an investor to purchase two thousand shares for $62,000. In March 2024, the stock was trading at $81 per share, making that $62,000 invested worth $162,000. These

calculations assume that the $100,000 is the only source of income for each tax-payer. The difference would be even starker if they had other sources of income, as wage income can be taxed at rates as high as 37 percent and payroll taxes are imposed at 15.3 percent. Meanwhile, the top rate on capital gains is 20 percent.

23. Heidi Chung, "The Stock Market's Biggest Winners and Losers of the Past Decade," Yahoo! Finance, December 4, 2019, https://finance.ya hoo.com/news/the-stock-markets-biggest-winners-and-losers-of-the-past -decade-141103073.html.

24. Adam Hayes, "Accredited Investor: Duties and Requirements," Investope-dia, June 2, 2024, https://www.investopedia.com/terms/a/accreditedinvestor.asp.

25. Taxes on these gains can be put off even later through the use of one of several provisions that allow further deferral of capital gains, including like-kind exchanges and investments in opportunity zones.

26. Moore v. United States, 602 U.S. 572 (2024).

27. Some tax scholars have pointed out that the same can be said about realized gains, as proceeds from sales can also be invested in ways that can then lose value.

28. See, e.g., William D. Andrews, "The Achilles' Heel of the Compre-hensive Income Tax," in *New Directions in Federal Tax Policy for the 1980s*, ed. Charles E. Walker and Mark A. Bloomfield (American Council for Capital Formation, 1983), 278–85.

29. Marjorie E. Kornhauser, "The Story of Macomber: The Continuing Legacy of Realization," in *Tax Stories: An In-Depth Look at Ten Leading Federal Income Tax Cases* (Foundation Press, 2009), https://ssrn.com/abstract=316483.

30. David M. Schizer, "Realization as Subsidy," *New York University Law Review* 73, no. 5 (November 1998): 1549–626.

31. As one prominent tax scholar described it: "Deferral of gain is not as serious as outright exemption, but it is the next best thing, as sophisticated taxpayers and their counsel are now well aware. Deferral for a generation, in a 6 percent world is tantamount to three-fourths exemption. In a 12 percent world, it is tantamount to fifteen-sixteenths exemption. Furthermore, the omission of unrealized appreciation and its correlatives can be magnified by le-verage to produce exemptions from income way beyond mere accumulation." Andrews, "The Achilles' Heel of the Comprehensive Income Tax," 278–85.

32. Some qualified retirement plans and IRAs allow many working Ameri-cans to enjoy the benefit of deferral for at least a small portion of their in-come. However, they pay for it in the end through the rules that provide that the full value of property set aside is taxed at ordinary income rates.

33. For a full report on these proposals, see American College of Trust and Estate Counsel (ACTEC), *Report by the ACTEC Tax Policy Study Committee*

on Proposals to Tax the Deemed Realization of Gain on Gratuitous Transfers of Appreciated Property, October 15, 2019, https://www.actec.org/wp-content/up loads/2023/08/Submission-ACTEC_Deemed_Realization_Report_-10-15-19. pdf. The proposals are also discussed on ACTEC, "Deemed Realization of Gains on Gratuitous Transfers," *ACTEC Trust & Estate Talk* (podcast), episode 82, November 2019, https://actecfoundation.org/podcasts/deemed-realization -tax/. Finally, this proposal has also been put forth by several tax scholars, includ- ing Lawrence Zelenak, "Taxing Gains at Death," *Vanderbilt Law Review* 46, no. 2 (March 1993), https://scholarship.law.vanderbilt.edu/vlr/vol46/iss2/3/; Joseph M. Dodge, "A Deemed Realization Approach Is Superior to Carryover Basis (and Avoids Most of the Problems of the Estate and Gift Tax)," *Tax Law Review* 54 (2001): 421–554; Samuel D. Brunson, "Afterlife of the Death Tax," *Indiana Law Journal* 94, no. 2 (2019): 355–88; Jeffrey L. Kwall, "When Should Asset Apprecia- tion Be Taxed? The Case for a Disposition Standard of Realization," *Indiana Law Journal* 86 (February 2010), http://dx.doi.org/10.2139/ssrn.1558610.

34. "The Power of Dividends: Past, Present, and Future," Hartford Funds, January 4, 2024, https://www.hartfordfunds.com/insights/market -perspectives/equity/the-power-of-dividends.html.

35. "Dow Jones—DJIA—100 Year Historical Chart," Macrotrends, 2024, https://www.macrotrends.net/1319/dow-jones-100-year-historical-chart.

36. 17 C.F.R. 240 (Release No. 33-6434; 34-19244; IC-12823), Purchases of Certain Equity Securities by the Issuer and Others; Adoption of Safe Harbor, 47 Fed. Reg. 228 (Nov. 26, 1982).

37. Roni Michaely and Amani Moin, "Disappearing and Reappearing Div- idends," *Journal of Financial Economics*, June 27, 2021, https://www.science direct.com/science/article/abs/pii/S0304405X21002993.

38. According to a 2015 Reuters special report: "As corporate America engages in an unprecedented buyback binge, soaring CEO pay tied to short- term performance measures like EPS is prompting criticism that executives are using stock repurchases to enrich themselves at the expense of long- term corporate health, capital investment and employment." Karen Brettell, David Gaffen, and David Rohde, "Stock Buybacks Enrich the Bosses Even When Business Sags," Reuters Investigates, December 10, 2015, https://www .reuters.com/investigates/special-report/usa-buybacks-pay/.

39. Alfred Rappaport, "New Thinking on How to Link Executive Pay with Performance," *Harvard Business Review*, March–April 1999, https://hbr .org/1999/03/new-thinking-on-how-to-link-executive-pay-with-performance.

40. Amit Batish, "Associated Press CEO Pay Study," Equilar, June 3, 2024, https://www.equilar.com/reports/110-equilar-associated-press-ceo-pay -study-2024.html.

41. This phrase was coined by the law professor Edward McCaffery.

42. Rachel Louise Ensign and Richard Rubin, "Buy, Borrow, Die: How Rich Americans Live Off Their Paper Wealth," *Wall Street Journal*, July 13, 2021, https://www.wsj.com/articles/buy-borrow-die-how-rich-americans -live-off-their-paper-wealth-11625909583.

43. Antonio Pequeño IV, "Billionaires Jeff Bezos and Larry Ellison Battling for World's 2nd Richest Person," *Forbes*, November 14, 2024, https:// www.forbes.com/sites/antoniopequenoiv/2024/11/14/billionaires-jeff-bezos -and-larry-ellison-battling-for-worlds-2nd-richest-person/; Brian O'Connell and Dominic Diongson, "Larry Ellison's Net Worth: Salary & Multibillionaire Status from Oracle Stake," *The Street*, January 30, 2024, https://www .thestreet.com/lifestyle/larry-ellison-net-worth-15100634.

44. Sophie Alexander, "Losing Paradise," *Bloomberg Businessweek*, June 13, 2022.

45. TRD Staff, "Billionaire Ellison Turning Hawaii's Lanai into 'Playground for the Rich,'" *The Real Deal*, June 12, 2022, https://therealdeal.com /new-york/2022/06/12/billionaire-ellison-turning-hawaiis-lanai-into-play ground-for-the-rich/.

46. *Forbes* noted that 232 of the 400 billionaires on its list had their wealth primarily in private firms. Of the 168 remaining billionaires, *Forbes* found that 32 had pledged substantial amounts of stock. John Hyatt, "How America's Richest People Can Access Billions Without Selling Their Stock," *Forbes*, November 11, 2021, https://www.forbes.com/sites/johnhyatt/2021/11/11 /how-americas-richest-people-larry-ellison-elon-musk-can-access-billions -without-selling-their-stock/, as cited in Edward G. Fox and Zachary D. Liscow, "No More Tax-Free Lunch for Billionaires: Closing the Borrowing Loophole," *Tax Notes Federal* 182, no. 4 (February 2024): 647, https://ssrn .com/abstract=471619.

47. Jun Frank, "Share Pledges Lose Popularity as Companies Clamp Down," *Institutional Shareholder Services Insights*, May 10, 2022, https:// insights.issgovernance.com/posts/share-pledges-lose-popularity-as-com panies-clamp-down/. See also Albert Vanderlaan, Soo Hwang, and Cynthia Angell, "Considerations for Company Insiders When Contemplating Pledging Shares," *Orrick Insights*, January 19, 2023, https://www.orrick .com/en/Insights/2023/01/Considerations-for-Company-Insiders-When -Contemplating-Pledging-Shares; Hyatt, "How America's Richest People Can Access Billions"; Blake Schmidt, Pei Yi Mak, Venus Feng, and Tom Metcalf, "Wealthy Facing Margin Calls Show Pitfalls of Pledged Shares," *Bloomberg*, March 20, 2020, https://www.bloomberg.com/news/articles/2020-03-19 /wealthy-facing-margin-calls-show-pitfalls-of-pledged-shares.

48. Associated Press, "Green Mountain Founder Says He Was Caught Off-Guard," *Telegram*, May 9, 2012, https://www.telegram.com/story/news/local/south-west/2012/05/09/green-mountain-founder-says-he/49641488007/; Peter Eavis, "Green Mountain Replaces Chairman After Margin Call," *New York Times DealBook*, May 8, 2012, https://archive.nytimes.com/dealbook.nytimes.com/2012/05/08/green-mountain-replaces-chairman-after-margin-call/; James O'Toole, "Green Mountain Chair Out After Trading Violation," *CNN Money*, May 8, 2012, https://money.cnn.com/2012/05/08/news/companies/green-mountain-chairman/index.htm.

49. Cara Lombardo, "Carl Icahn Gets Breathing Room from Lenders Following Short-Seller Attack," *Wall Street Journal*, July 10, 2023, https://www.wsj.com/articles/carl-icahn-gets-breathing-room-from-lenders-following-short-seller-attack-7f44133c; John Hyatt, "Hedge Fund Billionaire Carl Icahn Lost over $6 Billion Yesterday," *Forbes*, May 3, 2023, https://www.forbes.com/sites/johnhyatt/2023/05/03/hedge-fund-billionaire-carl-icahn-lost-over-6-billion-yesterday/.

50. Frank, "Share Pledges Lose Popularity." See also Hyatt, "How America's Richest People Can Access Billions Without Selling Their Stock."

51. Frank, "Share Pledges Lose Popularity." See also Hyatt, "How America's Richest People Can Access Billions"; Vanderlaan et al., "Considerations for Company Insiders."

52. Hyatt, "How America's Richest People Can Access Billions"; Devon Pendleton and Tom Maloney, "Billionaire Duo Keeps Danaher Grip While Giving $3.3 Billion," *Bloomberg*, June 29, 2021, https://www.bloomberg.com/news/articles/2021-06-29/billionaire-duo-keeps-danaher-grip-while-doling-out-3-3-billion.

53. Kinder Morgan Inc., *Stock Ownership Guidelines for Directors and Executive Officers* (Kinder Morgan Inc, 2020), 1–2, https://www.kindermorgan.com/WWWKM/media/AboutUs/documents/Stock_Ownership_Guidelines.pdf.

54. Hyatt, "How America's Richest People Can Access Billions."

55. Tax Policy Center, "What Is the Effect of a Lower Tax Rate for Capital Gains?," *The Tax Policy Briefing Book*, https://taxpolicycenter.org/briefing-book/what-effect-lower-tax-rate-capital-gains.

56. "I earned money the old fashioned way: I inherited it" was the line of Republican candidate John Raese, who frequently ran for Senate and other high political offices in West Virginia between 1984 and 2012, most recently losing to Senator Joe Manchin. Jim McKay, "Gov. Joe Manchin Campaign Launches Strong New Ad vs. John Raese," *HuffPost*, September 30, 2010, https://www.huffpost.com/entry/gov-joe-manchin-campaign_b_744450. A

similar sentiment is captured by this comment: "How did I get my million dollars? It was simple. One day, I bought an apple for a nickel. That night, I cleaned and polished it. The next day, I sold it for a dime. With that dime, I bought two apples. That night, I cleaned and polished them, and sold them the next day for twenty cents. I repeated that process every day, without fail, until I had amassed $6.40, whereupon my grandfather died and left me $999,994 in his will." "Why Are People So Ashamed About Inheriting Money?," *Financial Samurai* (blog), August 21, 2021, https://www.financial samurai.com/why-are-people-so-ashamed-about-inheriting-money/.

57. Even *Forbes* magazine gives short shrift to the enormous number of inheritors on that list: "The Forbes 400 remains a list of self-made multi-billionaires, with 279, or 70%, of the 2023 listees having created their fortune rather than inheriting it." Chase Peterson-Withorn, "The 2023 Forbes 400 List of Richest Americans: Facts and Figures," *Forbes*, March 7, 2024, https://www.forbes.com/sites/chasewithorn/2023/10/03 /the-2023-forbes-400-list-of-richest-americans-facts-and-figures/.

58. The U.S. Code (26 U.S.C. 102) provides that gross income does not include the value of property acquired by gift, bequest, devise, or inheritance.

59. Richard Schmalbeck, "Gifts and the Income Tax—An Enduring Puzzle," *Law and Contemporary Problems* 73 (Winter 2010): 63–93, https://schol arship.law.duke.edu/lcp/vol73/iss1/4.

60. Although Schmalbeck, in "Gifts and the Income Tax," argues in favor of this exclusion, many other tax scholars have taken the position that there are no valid policy justifications. See Henry C. Simons, *Personal Income Taxation* (University of Chicago Press, 1938), 56–58; Joseph M. Dodge, "Beyond Estate and Gift Tax Reform: Including Gifts and Bequests in Income," *Harvard Law Review* 91 (1978): 1177–211; William Klein, "An Enigma in the Federal Income Tax: The Meaning of the Word 'Gift,'" *Minnesota Law Review* 48 (1963): 215–63; Marjorie E. Kornhauser, "The Constitutional Meaning of Income and the Income Taxation of Gifts," *Connecticut Law Review* 25 (1992): 28–37; Lawrence Zelenak, "The Reasons for a Consumption Tax and the Income Taxation of Gifts" (commentary), *Tax Law Review* 51 (1996): 601–3, qtd. in Douglas A. Kahn, "The Taxation of a Gift or Inheritance from an Employer," *Tax Law* 64, no. 2 (2011): 273–300, at n. 7, https://repository .law.umich.edu/cgi/viewcontent.cgi?article=2201&context=articles.

61. Mark Maremont and Leslie Scism, "Shift to Wealthier Clientele Puts Life Insurers in a Bind," *Wall Street Journal*, October 3, 2010, https://www .wsj.com/articles/SB10001424052748703435104575421411449555240.

62. Ron Wyden, "Private Placement Life Insurance Needs More Oversight," *Tax Notes*, February 21, 2024, https://www.taxnotes.com

/research/federal/legislative-documents/congressional-news-releases
/private-placement-life-insurance-needs-more-oversight-wyden-says/7j7lq.

63. For the 2024 Tax Expenditure Budget, at https://home.treasury.gov
/system/files/131/Tax-Expenditures-FY2024.pdf.

CHAPTER THREE

1. David Kocieniewski, "Legacy for One Billionaire: Death, but No Taxes," *New York Times*, June 8, 2010, https://www.nytimes.com/2010/06/09 /business/09estate.html.

2. Mark Luscombe, "Historical Look at Estate and Gift Tax Rates," Wolters Kluwer, March 9, 2022, https://www.wolterskluwer.com/en /expert-insights/whole-ball-of-tax-historical-estate-and-gift-tax-rates.

3. Although President Bush wanted to provide permanent repeal of the estate tax, he was limited by the Byrd Rule, which required a sixty-vote majority in the Senate for legislation that increased the federal deficit beyond a ten-year term. To address this, the Economic Growth and Tax Reconciliation Act of 2001 (EGTRRA), H.R. 1836, 107th Cong. (2001–2), gradually increased the estate tax exemption from 2001 to 2009 and repealed the estate tax in 2010. Then, EGTRA sunsetted on January 1, 2011, and estate tax laws returned to how they were before EGTRA. This same reason is why President Trump's 2016 tax law sunsetted at the end of 2025.

4. "5 Billionaires Who Skated on a Death Tax," *CNN Money*, December 22, 2010, https://money.cnn.com/galleries/2010/news/economy/1012/gallery.bil lionaires_tax_holiday.fortune/index.html.

5. Samuel D. Brunson, "Afterlife of the Death Tax," *Indiana Law Journal* 94, no. 2 (2019): 355–88, https://www.repository.law.indiana.edu/ilj/vol94 /iss2/1.

6. As the legal historian Ganesh Sitaraman wrote in *The Crisis of the Middle-Class Constitution* (Alfred A. Knopf, 2017), "The ability to pass on wealth to the next generation was one of the founders' great fears" (256).

7. The American aversion to aristocracy developed long before the Fourteenth Amendment and is, of course, reflected elsewhere in the Constitution. U.S. Const., art. I, § 9, cl. 8 ("No Title of Nobility shall be granted by the United States"). See also Virginia Declaration of Rights (1776), in Robert Rutland, *The Birth of the Bill of Rights 1776–1791* (University of North Carolina Press, 1955), app. A ("no man, or set of men, are entitled to exclusive or separate emoluments or privileges from the community, but in consideration of public[] services"); Zobel v. Williams, 457 U.S. 55 (1982).

8. Lester J. Cappon, ed., *The Adams-Jefferson Letters: The Complete Correspondence Between Thomas Jefferson and Abigail and John Adams* (University of North Carolina Press, 1959), 2:387–92, available at https://press-pubs .uchicago.edu/founders/documents/v1ch15s61.html.

9. From 1776 to 1779, Jefferson served as a member of the Virginia House of Delegates, where he successfully sought to abolish entail and primogeniture, legal devices that preserved land estates and passed them on to eldest sons, exclusive of any other family members, upon the father's death. Jefferson's efforts to abolish primogeniture would strike a blow to inherited concentrations of wealth. It was a difficult fight, but he eventually prevailed. Peter Onuf, "Thomas Jefferson: Life Before the Presidency," UVA Miller Center, https://millercenter.org/president/jefferson/life-before-the -presidency. See also Lee Alston and Morton Schapiro, "Inheritance Laws Across Colonies: Causes and Consequences," *Journal of Economic History* 44, no. 2 (June 1984): 277–87, https://www.jstor.org/stable/2120705.

10. Primogeniture applied to wills; Jefferson also worked to abolish the fee tail, which was a mode of transferring property that automatically passed title upon death to the next eligible eldest male heir.

11. Alexis de Tocqueville, "That Amongst the Americans All Honest Callings Are Honorable," in *Democracy in America*, trans. Henry Reeve, Esq. (Saunders and Otley, 1835), https://www.gutenberg.org/files/815/815 -h/815-h.htm.

12. Steven Mintz and Sara McNeil, "Overview of the Gilded Age," Digital History, ID 2916, https://www.digitalhistory.uh.edu/era.cfm?eraid =9&smtid=1.

13. The time was described by the historian Gary Gerstle, in *The Rise and Fall of Neoliberal Order: America and the World in the Free Market Era* (Oxford University Press, 2022), as one of "stunning technological breakthrough and industrial creativity giving way to monopoly, corruption and inequality" (168).

14. The only tax on inheritances in this era was from 1898 to 1902. The War Revenue Act of 1898 applied only to personal, not real, property and had a top rate of 15 percent. Darien Jacobson, Brian Raub, and Barry Johnson, "The Estate Tax: Ninety Years and Counting," IRS, https://www.irs.gov/pub /irs-soi/ninetyestate.pdf.

15. The historian Steve Fraser appears in the 2018 PBS documentary "The Gilded Age," *American Experience*, at 1:48:43. The episode is available at YouTube, https://www.youtube.com/watch?v=yjpYzFtxfjU.

16. Gerhard Peters and John T. Woolley, "Populist Party Platform of 1892," The American Presidency Project, https://www.presidency.ucsb.edu /node/273285.

17. Sidney Ratner, *Taxation and Democracy in America* (John Wiley & Sons, 1967), 254.

18. E. L. Godkin, "An Able Englishman's View," *New York Evening Post* (1900), as quoted in Sarah Churchwell, "A Brief History of the American Dream," *The Catalyst: A Journal of Ideas from the Bush Institute* 21 (Winter 2021): https://www.bushcenter.org/catalyst/state-of-the-american-dream/churchwell-history-of-the-american-dream.

19. U.S. Const., art. I, § 9, cl. 8: "No Title of Nobility shall be granted by the United States: And no Person holding any Office of Profit or Trust under them, shall, without the Consent of the Congress, accept of any present, Emolument, Office, or Title, of any kind whatever, from any King, Prince, or foreign State."

20. One of the most famous of these was Consuelo Vanderbilt, heir to the Vanderbilt fortune, whose mother pressured her into marrying the Ninth Duke of Marlborough.

21. Thorstein Veblen, *The Theory of the Leisure Class* (Macmillan Co., 1899); Georgios Patsiaouras and James Fitchett, "The Evolution of Conspicuous Consumption," *Journal of Historical Research in Marketing* 4, no. 1 (January 2012): 154–76. See also Michael McGerr, *A Fierce Discontent: The Rise and Fall of the Progressive Movement in America* (Oxford University Press, 2005), 245; "Some New York Palaces," *Harper's Weekly*, April 7, 1894; John Tauranac, *Elegant New York: The Builders and the Buildings* (Abbeville Press, 1985), 116; "The Vanderbilt Palaces," *New York Times*, August 25, 1881, 3; "The Vanderbilt Houses," *Harper's Weekly 26*, January 21, 1882, 42.

22. Renee Rosen, "Gilded Age Parties Were Even Wilder Than You Can Imagine," *LitHub* (blog), April 22, 2021, https://lithub.com/gilded-age-parties-were-even-wilder-than-you-can-imagine/.

23. McGerr, *Fierce Discontent*, 152.

24. Ratner, *Taxation and Democracy in America*, 235.

25. Ratner, *Taxation and Democracy in America*, 235.

26. Ratner, *Taxation and Democracy in America*, 235.

27. W. Elliot Brownlee, *Federal Taxation in America*, 3rd ed. (Cambridge University Press, 2016), 83.

28. Andrew Carnegie, "The Gospel of Wealth," in *The Gospel of Wealth and Other Timely Essays*, ed. Andrew C. Kirkland (1962), https://www.carnegie.org/about/our-history/gospelofwealth/.

29. In the words of Carnegie in "The Gospel of Wealth": "We accept and welcome, therefore, as conditions to which we must accommodate ourselves, great inequality of environment, the concentration of business, industrial and commercial, in the hands of a few, and the law of competition between

these, as being not only beneficial, but essential for the future progress of the race." Carnegie, "Gospel of Wealth."

30. As Carnegie went on to explain: "This is not wealth, but only competence which it should be the aim of all to acquire." Carnegie, "Gospel of Wealth."

31. Carnegie, "Gospel of Wealth."

32. Carnegie, "Gospel of Wealth."

33. Ratner, *Taxation and Democracy in America*, 236.

34. According to Ratner, *Taxation and Democracy in America*, 236.

35. "For an Inheritance Tax as Check on Rich," *Wall Street Journal*, October 26, 1907.

36. Kenneth Scheve and David Stasavage, *Taxing the Rich* (Princeton University Press, 2016), 100.

37. John Ashworth, *Agrarians & Aristocrats: Party Political Ideology in the United States, 1837–1846* (Cambridge University Press, 1987), 252; Harold C. Syrett, ed., *The Papers of Alexander Hamilton*, vol. 10, *December 1791–January 1792* (Columbia University Press, 1966), 230–340.

38. William T. Horner, *Ohio's Kingmaker: Mark Hanna, Man and Myth* (Ohio University Press, 2010), 179; John E. Pixton Jr., *Charles G. Dawes and the McKinley Campaign* (University of Illinois Press, 1955), 300–301; Joan Waugh, "The Election of 1896," *Gilded Age Politics* (blog), https://www.ss cnet.ucla.edu/history/waughj/classes/gildedage/private/gilded_age_politics /history/election_of_1896.html, citing Paul F. Boller, *Presidential Campaigns* (Oxford University Press, 2004), 167–69.

39. J. S. Pughe captured the power of the Dingley Tariff in a cartoon titled "The political Barbara Frietchie." The cartoon is available at https:// en.wikipedia.org/wiki/Dingley_Act#/media/File:The_political_Barbara _Frietchie_-_J.S._Pughe._LCCN2011645678.jpg. For more discussion of the economic harm caused by tariffs, see Matthew Rooney, "Tariffs Are Great—If You Like Raising Prices, Undermining Jobs, and Inhibiting Innovation," *The Catalyst: A Journal of Ideas from the Bush Institute* 12 (Fall 2018): https://www .bushcenter.org/catalyst/opportunity-road/rooney-tariffs-rising-prices; Erica York, "Separating Tariff Facts from Tariff Fictions," *Cato Institute*, April 16, 2024, https://www.cato.org/publications/separating-tariff-facts-tariff-fictions.

40. Theodore Roosevelt, "True American Ideals," *The Forum* (February, 1895), 744.

41. Ratner, *Taxation and Democracy in America*, 259.

42. Amy Tikkanen, "Leon Czolgosz: American Assassin," in *Encyclopaedia Britannica*, 2025, https://www.britannica.com/biography/Leon-Czolgosz.

43. Elizabeth McKillen, "The Socialist Party of America, 1900–1929," *Oxford Research Encyclopedia of American History* (June 2017), https://oxfordre.com/americanhistory/view/10.1093/acrefore/9780199329175.001.0001/acrefore-9780199329175-e-413.

44. James Weinstein, *The Decline of Socialism in America, 1912–1925* (Vintage Books, 1969), 116–18, tables 2 and 3.

45. McKillen, "Socialist Party of America."

46. "As he later explained: very large fortunes are needless and useless, for they make no one really happy and increase no one's usefulness, and furthermore they do infinite harm and they contain the threat of far greater harm." Louis Eisenstein, "The Rise and Decline of the Estate Tax," *Tax Law Review* 11 (1956): 223–60, at 228.

47. McGerr, *Fierce Discontent*, 98.

48. Ratner, *Taxation and Democracy in America*, 342.

49. Pollock v. Farmer's Loan & Trust Co. (1895), 157 U.S. 429 (1895). The case was affirmed on rehearing at 158 U.S. 601 (1895).

50. Mark Luscombe, "Historical Income Tax Rates," Wolters Kluwer, December 30, 2022, https://www.wolterskluwer.com/en/expert-insights/whole-ball-of-tax-historical-income-tax-rates.

51. Rates were originally 10 percent but soon increased to 25 percent to fund World War I. Luscombe, "Historical Income Tax Rates."

52. In 1913, taxes on commodities in the country or at its ports yielded 94.6 percent of all federal revenues. In 1930, taxes on personal and corporation incomes yielded 66.5 percent of all federal revenues. Ratner, *Taxation and Democracy in America*, 308–9.

53. Scheve and Stasavage present the results of this study in *Taxing the Rich*.

54. Scheve and Stasavage, *Taxing the Rich*, 5.

55. The first national conscription was in 1917 to fight World War I; the country then adopted its first peacetime draft in 1970. The last conscription was in 1975, which coincides with the height of taxing the wealthy. "Historical Timeline," Selective Service System, https://www.sss.gov/history-and-records/timeline/.

56. Bernard Rostker, "50 Years Without the Draft," *AUSA: Association of the United States Army*, June 21, 2023, https://www.ausa.org/articles/50-years-without-draft-behind-bold-move-ended-conscription-and-whats-next-all-volunteer.

57. Ajay Mehrotra, "Lawyers, Guns and Public Moneys: The U.S. Treasury, World War I, and the Administration of the Modern Fiscal State.

Forum: World War I and the Making of the Modern American Fiscal State," *Law & History Review* 28 (2010): 173, 185.

58. Brownlee, *Federal Taxation*, 94.

59. "The social necessity for breaking up large fortunes in this country does not exist. Very wisely our forefathers declined to implant in this country the principle of primogeniture under which the eldest son alone inherited and kept the properties intact. Under our American law, it is customary for estates to be divided equally among the children; and in a few generations any single large fortune is split into many moderate inheritances. As a usual thing, the continuation of a single fortune through several generations has been proven to be impossible. It is an often quoted saying that 'there are three generations from shirt sleeves to shirt sleeves.' To recapitulate: the estate tax furnishes but a slight portion of the revenues to the Federal Government but it supplies a large and important part of the State revenues. To destroy values from which the States receive income is to force them to resort to higher taxes on land." Andrew W. Mellon, *Taxation: The People's Business* (Macmillan Co., 1924), 123–24.

60. "Mellon Family," *Forbes*, https://www.forbes.com/profile/mellon/.

61. Eisenstein, "The Rise and Decline of the Estate Tax," 234.

62. Herbert Hoover, "Reform in Some Federal Taxes," in *Addresses Upon the American Road 1933–1938* (Scribner's Sons, 1936), 78.

63. Franklin D. Roosevelt, "Message to Congress on Tax Revision," The American Presidency Project, https://www.presidency.ucsb.edu/documents /message-congress-tax-revision.

64. Roosevelt, "Message to Congress."

65. David Joulfaian, *The Federal Estate Tax: History, Law, and Economics* (MIT Press, 2019), 18.

66. Some of the tools used to avoid taxes are outlined in the ProPublica story on leaked tax returns: Patricia Callahan, James Bandler, Justin Elliott, Doris Burke, and Jeff Ernsthausen, "The Great Inheritors: How Three Families Shielded Their Fortunes from Taxes for Generations" ProPublica, December 15, 2021, https://www.propublica.org/article/the-great-inheritors -how-three-families-shielded-their-fortunes-from-taxes-for-generations. The value of the Mars family assets in 2024 was reported by Abigail Summerville, "Mars' Biggest Deal Clinched by Secretive, Deep-Pocketed Family," *Reuters*, August 15, 2024, https://www.reuters.com/markets/deals /mars-biggest-deal-clinched-by-secretive-deep-pocketed-family-2024 -08-14.

67. Hillary Hoffower and Sarah Jackson, "Meet the Mars Family, Heirs to the Snickers and M&M's Candy Empire, Who Avoided the Limelight

for Years," *Business Insider*, May 20, 2024, https://www.businessinsider.com
/mars-inc-family-fortune-net-worth-lifestyle-snickers-twix-2019-3.

68. Summerville, "Mars' Biggest Deal."

69. Jan Pottker, "From the Archives: Sweet Secrets: Opening Doors
on the Very Private Lives of the Billionaire Mars Family," *The Washingtonian*, April 29, 2008, https://www.washingtonian.com/2008/04/29/from-the
-archives-sweet-secrets-opening-doors-on-the-very-private-lives-of-the-bil
lionaire-mars-fami/.

70. The first version of the generation-skipping transfer tax was enacted
in 1976, however, the tax was significantly revised and eventually replaced
with a new version in 1986.

71. For some examples of how this is done, see Jesse Drucker, "Death
and Taxes," *New York Times*, December 5, 2024, https://www.nytimes
.com/2024/12/05/briefing/estate-taxes.html.

72. Chapter 14 of the Internal Revenue Code (i.e., §§2701–4) became law
in 1990. Chapter 14, "Special Valuation Rules," specifically pertains to the
federal estate, gift, and generation-skipping transfer taxes. The adoption of
these sections was an attempt by Congress to eliminate the use of valuation
discounts for tax planning and compliance purposes.

73. Gerstle, *Rise and Fall of the Neoliberal Order*, 39, 41–46.

74. Gerstle, *Rise and Fall of the Neoliberal Order*, 108–15.

75. Molly Ball, "The Agony of Frank Luntz," *The Atlantic*, January 6, 2014, https://www.theatlantic.com/politics/archive/2014/01
/the-agony-of-frank-luntz/282766/.

76. Frank Luntz, *Words That Work: It's Not What You Say, It's What People
Hear* (Hyperion, 2007).

77. Mark Abadi, "Republicans Say 'Death Tax' While Democrats Say 'Estate Tax'—And There's a Fascinating Reason Why," *Business Insider*, October 19,
2017, https://www.businessinsider.com/death-tax-or-estate-tax-2017-10. See
also Luntz, *Words That Work*.

78. Michael J. Graetz and Ian Shapiro, *Death by a Thousand Cuts: The
Fight over Taxing Inherited Wealth* (Princeton University Press, 2006).

79. Joint Economic Committee, US Congress, *The Economics of the Estate
Tax*, December 1998, https://www.jec.senate.gov/public/index.cfm/1998/12
/report-11d82efd-68c0-4d92-8abd-3fceb5ae627f. For Chester Thigpen's story,
see p. 44 of the report.

80. Public Citizen's Congress Watch and United for a Fair Economy,
*Spending Millions to Save Billions: The Campaign of the Super Wealthy to Kill
the Estate Tax* (April 2006), 24, https://www.citizen.org/wp-content/uploads
/estatetaxfinal.pdf.

81. I myself wrote some, including this one: Ray Madoff, "Protect the Farm, Tax the Manor," *New York Times*, November 21, 2009, https://www.nytimes.com/2009/11/21/opinion/21madoff.html.

82. Luntz suggested calling this "the quicksand theory of taxation communication," and in Luntzian fashion, he went on to describe why this phrase would likely stick: "Because 'taxation' and 'communication' rhyme people will remember. Also the word *quicksand* is very visual. And a great fear. It's how people don't want to die." Luntz, *Words That Work*, n.p.

83. John Miller, "The Paris Hilton Tax Break," *National Review*, August 4, 2008, https://www.nationalreview.com/corner/paris-hilton-tax-break-john-j-miller/.

84. Public Citizen's Congress Watch and United for a Fair Economy, *Spending Millions*.

85. For those covering the deaths of the rich and famous, it provided the opportunity for such reportorial punning as this: "George Steinbrenner, the irascible owner of the New York Yankees, hit the ball far over the fence (for tax purposes anyways) when he passed away on July 13, 2010, with a purported $1.1 billion estate. If he had died last year, the executors of George's estate could have faced federal estate taxes of almost $500 million, depending on how the estate was structured. However, since Mr. Steinbrenner died in 2010 (a year in which there may be no federal estate taxes), his heirs pitched the proverbial perfect game and escaped with a zero estate tax bill." Robert J. Kolasa, "George Steinbrenner's Estate Tax Homerun," *Trusts and Estates* (Illinois State Bar Association), October 2010, 1–5.

86. Joulfaian, *Federal Estate Tax*, 42.

87. Jane G. Gravelle, *The Estate and Gift Tax: An Overview*, Congressional Research Service, September 16, 2024, https://crsreports.congress.gov/product/pdf/R/R48183.

88. Helvering v. Gregory, 69 F. 2d 809, 810 (2nd Cir. 1934) (citations omitted), *aff'd*, Gregory v. Helvering, 293 U.S. 465 (1935).

89. The earliest problems arose with the original estate tax which applied only for transfers on death and not by gift. One notable beneficiary of this failure to tax gifts was the Rockefeller family, as John D. Rockefeller transferred an estimated $475 million of his fortune to his heirs between 1917 and 1922 by tax-free gift, an amount that would be worth over $8 billion today. But shortly thereafter, Congress closed the loophole by creating a gift tax. Today, the two taxes work together as part of an integrated system. William H. Gates Sr. and Chuck Collins, *Wealth and Our Commonwealth* (Beacon Press, 2003), 46.

CHAPTER FOUR

1. David Corn, "Secret Video: Romney Tells Millionaire Donors What He REALLY Thinks of Obama Voters," September 17, 2012, https://www .motherjones.com/politics/2012/09/secret-video-romney-private-fundraiser/. Mitt Romney wasn't the only Republican to complain about Americans who don't pay income taxes. In 2022, Senator Rick Scott from Florida proposed that "all Americans should pay some income tax to have skin in the game, even if a small amount. Currently over half of Americans pay no income tax." Howard Gleckman, "Scott's 'Skin in the Game' Plan Could Raise Taxes by $100 Billion in 2022, Mostly On Low- And Moderate-Income Households," Tax Policy Center, February 24, 2024, https://taxpolicycenter.org/taxvox /scotts-skin-game-plan-could-raise-taxes-100-billion-2022-mostly-low-and -moderate-income.

2. Domenico Montanaro, "Conservative Reaction Mixed to Rom- ney 47 Percent Video," NBC News, September 18, 2012, https://www .nbcnews.com/news/world/conservative-reaction-mixed-romney-47 -percent-video-flna1b5958500/. Romney eventually issued a general retrac- tion of his statement. Associated Press, "Romney on '47%': I Was 'Com- pletely Wrong,'" *USA Today*, October 5, 2012, https://www.usatoday .com/story/news/politics/2012/10/05/romney-47-percent-i-was-wrong /1614703/.

3. Romney quoted 47 percent as nonpayers, which appears to have been an approximation to align his argument with the percentage of voters supporting Obama. Corn, "Secret Video." See also "T22-0128—Tax Units with Zero or Negative Federal Individual Income Tax Under Current Law, 2011–2032," Tax Policy Center: Urban Institute and Brookings Institu- tion, October 27, 2022, https://www.taxpolicycenter.org/model-estimates /tax-units-with-zero-or-negative-federal-individual-income-tax-oct-2022 /t22-0128.

4. Self-employment taxes are imposed at a rate of 15.3 percent on the full $60,000, but income taxes are only calculated based on $55,410 (92.35 per- cent of net earnings from self-employment income). The reason for the lower amount is that when someone is employed by another, the employer contributes 7.65 percent of the tax for the employee and is able to deduct that amount from their income. See "Topic No. 554: Self-Employment Tax," IRS, https://www.irs.gov/taxtopics/tc554#:~:text=Generally%2C %20the%20amount%20subject%20to,from%20your%20trade%20or %20business.

5. One of the journalists who covered the march of Coxey's Army was Nelly Bly, among the most famous and intrepid reporters of the era. Bly had recently made her name by traversing the globe in a twenty-five-thousand -mile journey inspired by the fictional account from Jules Verne's *Around the World in Eighty Days*. Bly beat the fictional record and set the world record by completing the journey eight days ahead of schedule, in just seventy-two days. The entire country followed her daily updates in the *New York World*. She originally became known for her tough investigative work about New York's worst asylum, where she got herself committed to do firsthand reporting on the deplorable conditions.

6. "Grover Cleveland's Veto of the Texas Seed Bill," February 16, 1887, *American Yawp Reader*, https://www.americanyawp.com/reader/16-capital-and-labor /grover-clevelands-veto-of-the-texas-seed-bill-february-16-1887/.

7. See the video "Curator Talk—A Petition in Boots: The Legacy of Jacob Coxey's 1894 March on Washington," YouTube video, 55:15, posted by the Spurlock Museum of World Cultures, https://www.youtube.com /watch?v=wLJQQoi3VNk.

8. Fifty years later, on May 1, 1944, Coxey was invited back to the Capitol steps to finally give his speech to a world that had changed significantly in the interim.

9. "FDR's Statements on Social Security," Social Security Administration, https://www.ssa.gov/history/fdrstmts.html#message1.

10. "Historical Background and Development of Social Security," Social Security Administration, https://www.ssa.gov/history/briefhistory3 .html.

11. Gary Gerstle, review of *Mission from Moscow: American Communism in the 1930s*, by Harvey Klehr, *Reviews in American History* 12, no. 4 (1984): 559–66, https://doi.org/10.2307/2701913.

12. "Huey Long's Share Our Wealth Speech," *Huey Long: The Man, The Mission, and Legacy*, https://www.hueylong.com/programs/share-our-wealth -speech.php.

13. While Long would have been unlikely to beat Roosevelt on his own, there was great concern that he would be a spoiler and tip the election to the Republicans. Daniel J. B. Mitchell, "Townsend and Roosevelt: Lessons from the Struggle for Elderly Income Support," *Labor History* 42, no. 3 (2001): 255–76, https://doi.org/10.1080/00236560120068137.

14. Robert S. McElvaine, *The Depression and New Deal: A History in Documents* (Oxford University Press, 2003), 90.

15. Dennis W. Johnson, *The Laws That Shaped America: Fifteen Acts of Congress and Their Lasting Impact* (Routledge, 2009), 181.

16. Bruce Mason, "The Townsend Movement," *Southwestern Social Science Quarterly* 35, no. 1 (1954): 36–47, at 38.

17. In her memoir, *The Roosevelt I Knew* (Penguin Classics, 2011), Frances Perkins says that Roosevelt told her, "We have to have it [Social Security]. Congress can't stand the pressure of the Townsend Plan unless we have a real old-age insurance system" (294). As Roosevelt said, Social Security was passed by Congress substituting a pay-as-you-go "insurance" scheme for Townsend's far more generous pension plan, but as he told Perkins, it was the Townsend Clubs that forced Congress to act at all.

18. Roosevelt's original goal was for a simple plan in which "every child from the day he is born" is a "member of the social security system," but whatever the CES decided, "it should be based on the principle of social insurance and not be perceived as a form of welfare." Johnson, *Laws That Shaped America*, 184.

19. "Huey Long's Share Our Wealth Speech"; Johnson, *Laws That Shaped America*, 185.

20. Sven Steinmo, *Taxation and Democracy: Swedish, British and American Approaches to Financing the Modern State* (Yale University Press, 1993), 99, citing Martha Derthick, *Policymaking for Social Security* (Brookings Institution, 1979), 230.

21. Transcripts of Francis Perkins and George Sokolsky's statements from America's Town Meeting of the Air, "Should We Plan for Social Security?," December 19, 1935, Social Security Online, http://www.ssa.gov/history /1935radiodebate.html.

22. "Policy Basics: Top Ten Facts About Social Security," Center on Budget and Policy Priorities, May 31, 2024, https://www.cbpp.org/research /social-security/top-ten-facts-about-social-security.

23. The original 1935 legislation set up a plan that bore a much stronger resemblance to a private insurance plan, with the accumulation of a trust fund and the close alignment of contributions and benefits for any given cohort. The 1939 amendments, however, fundamentally changed the nature of the program. The amendments tied benefits to average earnings, initially over a minimum period of coverage, and added spousal and survivor benefits, which were effectively unfunded, thus breaking the link between lifetime contributions and benefits. Alicia H. Munnell, Wenliang Hou, and Geoffrey T. Sanzenbacher, "The Implications of Social Security's 'Missing Trust Fund,'" Center for Retirement Research at Boston College, June 4, 2019, https://crr.bc.edu/the-implications-of-social-securitys-missing-trust-fund/. Beginning in 1983, Congress revised Social Security to raise enough money to create a reserve. This is the reserve that is due to run out. "Policy Basics:

Understanding the Social Security Trust Funds," Center on Budget and Policy Priorities, July 24, 2024, https://www.cbpp.org/research/social-security /understanding-the-social-security-trust-funds-0.

24. Stephen C. Goss, "The Future Financial Status of the Social Security Program," *Social Security Bulletin* 70, no. 3 (2010): https://www.ssa.gov /policy/docs/ssb/v70n3/v70n3p111.html.

25. Flemming v. Nestor, 363 U.S. 603 (1960).

26. "The Ratio of Workers to Social Security Beneficiaries Is at a Low and Projected to Decline Further" Peter G. Peterson Foundation, August 4, 2022, https://www.pgpf.org/article/the-ratio-of-workers-to-social-security -beneficiaries-is-at-a-low-and-projected-to-decline-further/.

27. The retirement expert Alicia Munnell discusses the benefits of raising the wage base cap as a promising way to secure Social Security benefits going forward. Alicia Munnell, "To Fix Social Security, Increasing the Wage Base Should Be Part of the Solution," Center for Retirement Research at Boston College, August 12, 2024, https://crr.bc.edu/to-fix-social-security -increasing-the-wage-base-should-be-part-of-the-solution/.

28. As Edward McCaffery and Jonathan Baron explain, there are several reasons we are unlikely to recognize the full burden of payroll taxes. These include the facts that such taxes "are labeled 'contributions'; appear to be tied to social security and Medicare benefits; are matched by an employer 'share,' and so only appear at one-half their total level on employee pay stubs; require no onerous individual form completion; do not entail high marginal rates; are never manifest in a single lump sum due and payable at one time (say, April 15) to the ordinary taxpayer." Edward J. McCaffery and Jonathan Baron, "The Humpty Dumpty Blues: Disaggregation Bias in the Evaluation of Tax Systems," *Organizational Behavior and Human Decision Processes* 91, no. 2 (2003): 230–42, https://doi.org/10.1016/S0749-5978(03) 00026-8.

29. "Policy Basics: Federal Payroll Taxes," Center on Budget and Policy Priorities, October 25, 2022, https://www.cbpp.org/research/policy-basics -federal-payroll-taxes.

30. Taxpayers raising children may be able to offset some payroll taxes through the Earned Income Tax Credit or the Child Tax Credit.

31. The total tax is $4,590, although the employee will be able to deduct half of this amount from his income taxes.

32. This is the FICA wage cap for 2024. The 2.9 percent Medicare tax, in contrast, has no cap, and income in excess of $200,000 is subject to an additional tax of 0.9 percent paid only by the employee. See Rachel Blakely-Gray, "How to Calculate Payroll Taxes: A Look at Social Security and Medicare

Tax Calculations," Patriot Software, December 2, 2024, https://www.pa
triotsoftware.com/blog/payroll/how-calculate-payroll-taxes-for-employers/.

33. This regressivity of the payroll tax is offset in part by the fact that,
for those who eventually receive them, payments are mildly progressive. As
the Center on Budget and Policy Priorities explains in its "Policy Basics:
Federal Payroll Taxes": "Social Security benefits represent a higher propor-
tion of a worker's previous earnings for workers at lower earnings levels;
and while all Medicare beneficiaries are eligible for the same health care
services, high-income beneficiaries pay more in Medicare taxes and premiums. Low-income Medicare beneficiaries are also eligible for help paying for
their premiums and cost sharing. Variation in state laws and practices makes
it difficult to assess the distributional effect of unemployment insurance."

34. "Federal Revenue Trends over Time," in "How Much Revenue
Has the U.S. Government Collected This Year?," FiscalData.Treasury.
gov, 2024, https://fiscaldata.treasury.gov/americas-finance-guide/government
-revenue/.

CHAPTER FIVE

1. As reported by *Fortune*: "Though some equivocated over whether
to accept the invitation, regarding the trip as an inconvenience. But there
were the signatures at the bottom of the letter—from left to right, Rockefeller, Gates, Buffett. 'Impressive,' Eli Broad thought." Carol J. Loomis, "The
$600 Billion Challenge," *Fortune*, June 16, 2010, https://fortune.com/2010/06/16
/the-600-billion-challenge/?iid=sr-link1.

2. The letter was reported in Niall O'Dowd, "Secret Meeting of World's
Richest People Held in New York," Irish Central, May 18, 2009.

3. Luisa Kroll, "Billionaires 2008," *Forbes*, March 6, 2008 (updated July 16,
2012), https://www.forbes.com/forbes/2008/0324/080.html.

4. "About the Giving Pledge," Giving Pledge, https://givingpledge.org
/about.

5. Stephanie Strom, "Pledge to Give Away Fortunes Stirs Debate,"
New York Times, November 10, 2010, https://www.nytimes.com/2010/11/11
/giving/11PLEDGE.html. Gates was not the only one to describe it in a way
reminiscent of taxes. The initiative was later referred to by the *American
Prospect* as a "self-imposed wealth tax." Alexander Sammon, "The Billionaire
Class Created Their Own Wealth Tax. It Failed," *American Prospect*, November 18, 2019, https://prospect.org/power/billionaire-class-created-failed
-wealth-tax-giving-pledge/.

6. Robert Paine, "Are Charitable Pledges Legally Enforceable?," *Matters of Trust: Commentary on Trust Administration and Litigation* (blog), May 17, 2018, https://www.mattersoftrustlaw.com/2018/05/charitable-pledges-legally -enforceable/. Or as Ellen Remmer from Philanthropy Initiative said: "It can look like it's totally a P.R. thing, like they are royalty." Strom, "Pledge to Give Away Fortunes."

7. As Bill Ackman wrote in his letter accompanying his Giving Pledge: "In college, I had the opportunity to read John Rawls, and learn his methodology for determining how to organize the world. It made sense to me then, and still does. Rawls advised that you should imagine yourself in what he called 'the Original Position.' Pretend that you have not yet been born, and don't know to what family or in what country or circumstance you will find yourself. He argued that the world should be organized from such a vantage point. In other words, I believe the fairest distribution would require something along the lines of the Giving Pledge. Rawls proves that charitable giving is the right thing to do from an objectively fair vantage point." Cited in Ryan Vanzo, "Warren Buffett Wants You to Read These 3 Letters," Guru Focus (Yahoo Finance), September 22, 2016, https://finance.yahoo.com/news/warren-buffett-wants -read-3-202857799.html. Ackman may have come to reconsider his analysis as his letter is no longer available on the Giving Pledge site. "Bill Ackman and Neri Oxman," Giving Pledge, https://givingpledge.org/pledger?pledgerId=157.

8. Strom, "Pledge to Give Away Fortunes."

9. Peter Wilby, "The Rich Want a Better World? Try Paying Fair Wages and Tax," *The Guardian*, August 5, 2010.

10. Strom, "Pledge to Give Away Fortunes."

11. These savings are possible for a gift of appreciated property in which the donor has a zero cost basis and has enough ordinary income to be subject to tax at the highest marginal income tax rate. The income tax charitable deduction will save the donor 37 percent of the value of the gift; an additional 20 percent of the value of the contributed property if it is subject to capital gains taxes; and if the donor is subject to estate taxes, another 17 percent (40 percent of the remaining 43 percent) that would otherwise be remaining in the estate if no gift had been made. The tax benefits can be even more if the property is overvalued, a recurring issue for non-publicly-traded assets. Roger Colinvaux and Ray Madoff, "Charitable Tax Reform for the 21st Century," *TaxNotes* 164, no. 12 (2019): 1867–75, at 1867n1.

12. Alexis de Tocqueville, *Democracy in America*, trans. Henry Reeve, Esq. (Saunders and Otley, 1835), 596, https://www.gutenberg.org/files/815/815 -h/815-h.htm.

13. Victor Fleischer, "Stop Universities from Hoarding Money," *New

York Times, August 19, 2015, https://www.nytimes.com/2015/08/19/opin ion/stop-universities-from-hoarding-money.html. Harvard University, with its endowment in excess of $50 billion, is often described as a hedge fund with a university attached. See Astra Taylor, "Universities Are Becoming Billion-Dollar Hedge Funds with Schools Attached," *The Nation*, March 8, 2016, https://www.thenation.com/article/archive/universities-are-becoming -billion-dollar-hedge-funds-with-schools-attached/. "I was going to donate money to Yale. But maybe it makes more sense to mail a check directly to the hedge fund of my choice," Malcolm Gladwell tweeted last summer, causing a commotion that landed him on NPR. See "In Elite Schools' Vast Endowments, Malcolm Gladwell Sees 'Obscene' Inequity," *Weekend Edition Saturday* (NPR), August 22, 2015, https://www.npr.org/2015/08/22/433735934/in-elite-schools -vast-war-chests-malcolm-gladwell-sees-obscene-inequity. Many have also ques tioned whether hospitals deserve their charitable status, particularly when they engage in practices more suitable to businesses than charities. See Jessica Silver-Greenberg and Katie Thomas, "They Were Entitled to Free Care: Hospitals Hounded Them to Pay," *New York Times*, September 24, 2022, https://www .nytimes.com/2022/09/24/business/nonprofit-hospitals-poor-patients.html.

14. George Bush, "Address Accepting the Presidential Nomination at the Republican National Convention in New Orleans," August 18, 1998, American Presidency Project, https://www.presidency.ucsb.edu/documents /address-accepting-the-presidential-nomination-the-republican-national -convention-new.

15. Natalie Schwartz, "What Makes MacKenzie Scott's Gifts to Colleges Different from Other Donations," *Higher ED Dive*, December 18, 2020, https://www.highereddive.com/news/what-makes-mackenzie-scotts-gifts -to-colleges-different-from-other-donatio/592504/; Elizabeth Redden, "A Fairy Godmother for Once-Overlooked Colleges," *Inside Higher Ed*, January 3, 2021, https://www.insidehighered.com/news/2021/01/04/mackenzie-scott -surprises-hbcus-tribal-colleges-and-community-colleges-multimillion. For a list of Scott's donations, see https://yieldgiving.com/gifts/.

16. John A. Wallace and Robert W. Fisher, *The Charitable Deduction Under Section 170 of the Internal Revenue Code* (1977), 4:2131, in Research Papers Sponsored by the Commission on Private Philanthropy and Public Needs Filer Commission, 1964–80, Indianapolis Philanthropic Studies Archives, Indiana University, https://archives.iu.edu/catalog/mss024.

17. When taxpayers donate appreciated property, instead of money, to charity they are able to receive two levels of tax benefits for their charitable giving. Both types of donations reduce the person's taxable income (assuming the donor itemizes deductions as opposed to taking the standard deduction),

but donations of appreciated property also allow the donor to avoid the capital gains taxes that would be imposed if the property were sold. The effect of this double benefit is that a donor of cash can enjoy income tax benefits up to 37 percent of the value of the property, but a donor of appreciated property can enjoy tax benefits that are worth as much as 57 percent of the value of the property (37 percent for income tax purposes and 20 percent for capital gains purposes). This double tax benefit for contributions of appreciated property is one reason for the explosive growth of donor-advised funds, which facilitate this type of donation. The double benefit for contributions of appreciated property has long been questioned as a matter of logic and public policy. See Harry K. Mansfield and Ronald L. Groves, *Legal Aspects of Charitable Contributions of Appreciated Property to Public Charities*, 4:2251–60, Research Papers Sponsored by the Commission on Private Philanthropy and Public Needs Filer Commission, 1964–80, Indianapolis Philanthropic Studies Archives, Indiana University, https://archives.iu.edu/catalog/mss024. It could potentially be justified if there was added value to society or the charity from having direct donation of property (as when something particularly valuable is donated to a public museum). However, in most cases donations of property cause more trouble for the charity, which has to spend time and incur expenses to sell the property and extract cash to spend in support of its charitable mission.

18. The first federal estate tax was enacted in 1916. At the time, there was no exemption for charitable donations. However, after the adoption of the 1917 income tax, there was added pressure to add a similar exemption from estate taxes. In 1919, Congress authorized an estate tax deduction for bequests to charitable organizations. Revenue Act of 1918, ch. 18, tit. IV, §403(a)(3), 40 Stat. 1057 (1919). Unlike the income tax charitable deduction, there was no cap on the amount of deductible expenses, and the unlimited benefit continues today, though not without its critics. Professor Miranda Fleischer noted that "a coherent rationale for either the deduction's existence or its unlimited nature has never been fully developed in the legal literature," in contrast to "the rich literature exploring the income tax charitable deduction." Miranda Perry Fleischer, "Charitable Contributions in an Ideal Estate Tax," *Tax Law Review* 60 (2007): 263–321.

19. Andrew Lautz, "Tax Expenditures and the Budget, Explained," Bipartisan Policy Center, September 17, 2024, https://bipartisanpolicy.org/explainer/tax-expenditures-and-the-budget-explained/.

20. England explicitly uses this form of matching grants to fund its charities.

21. See Lautz, "Tax Expenditures," for tax expenditure information for 2024.

For total estate tax revenue, see "SOI Tax Stats—Collections and Refunds, by Type of Tax—IRS Data Book Table 1," IRS, https://www.irs.gov/statistics /soi-tax-stats-collections-and-refunds-by-type-of-tax-irs-data-book-table-1.

22. The capacity of a government to lure additional voluntary contributions for social welfare has become particularly tempting in an age when a combination of great concentrations of wealth and easy mobility of capital impedes the ability to impose high taxes. As a result, there is a growing trend for countries outside of the United States to add charitable tax incentives where previously they had none. OECD and Université de Genève, *Taxation and Philanthropy: Policy Brief* (2020), https://www.oecd.org/tax/tax-policy /policy-brief-taxation-and-philanthropy.pdf.

23. Rehabilitation Through the Arts and EveryMom Chicago are just two examples. For a broader sense, see the list of IRS-recognized charitable organizations: "Tax Exempt Organization Search," IRS, https://www.irs.gov /charities-non-profits/tax-exempt-organization-search.

24. Saul Levmore, "Taxes as Ballots," *University of Chicago Law Review* 65, no. 2 (1998): Art. 1, https://chicagounbound.uchicago.edu/uclrev/vol65 /iss2/1/. Although given the way our system currently allocates tax benefits— with 90 percent of Americans getting no tax benefits for their charitable donations—it is hard to justify this theory today.

25. These savings are possible for a gift of appreciated property in which the donor has a zero cost basis and is otherwise subject to income taxes at the highest marginal rate. The combination of income tax savings, capital gains tax savings and estate and gift tax savings could save a donor as much as 74 percent of the value of the donation. Colinvaux and Madoff, "Charitable Tax Reform," 1867n1.

26. Lilian Faulhaber, "The Hidden Limits of the Charitable Deduction: An Introduction to Hypersalience," *Boston University Law Review* 92 (2012): 1307–48, https://scholarship.law.bu.edu/faculty_scholarship/82. This conclusion has been both contested and supported in subsequent scholarship. See Jacob Goldin and Yair Listokin, "Tax Expenditure Salience," *American Law and Economics Review* 16 (2013): 144–76; Eric S. Smith, "Exploiting the Charitable Contribution Deduction's Hypersalience," *Utah Law Review* 2020, no. 2 (2020): https://doi.org/10.26054/0d-w27m-rs3m.

27. Alex Huntsberger, "12 Year-End Giving Statistics Every Fundraiser Should Know for 2024," Neon One, July 19, 2023, https://neonone.com /resources/blog/year-end-giving-statistics/.

28. Anna's self-employment payroll taxes will be imposed on her full $100,000 of income, but her income taxes will only be based on 92.35 percent of her income to account for the fact that, had she been employed by

someone else, her employer would be able to deduct the employer's portion of payroll taxes from the employer's income tax.

29. Scott Hodge, "Would Americans Make Charitable Donations Without Tax Incentives?," Tax Foundation, December 20, 2022, https://taxfounda tion.org/blog/charitable-deduction-tax-incentives/.

30. Some deductions that exceed this limit can be carried forward over five years, subject to the same income limitation. IRS, *Charitable Contributions* (Publication No. 526), 2023, https://www.irs.gov/pub/irs-pdf /p526.pdf.

31. This cap ranges from 20 percent to 60 percent of the donors' adjusted gross income, with the precise amount depending on the charitable recipient and whether the gift is of cash or property.

32. "About," Bill & Melinda Gates Foundation, https://www.gatesfounda tion.org/about. Emphasis added.

33. "Comments by Warren E. Buffett in Conjunction with His Annual Contribution of Berkshire Hathaway Shares to Five Foundations," *Business Wire*, June 23, 2021, https://www.businesswire.com/news/home /20210623005262/en/.

34. Theron Mohamed, "Warren Buffett Defends Himself After ProPublica Says He Avoids Taxes," *Markets Insider*, June 8, 2021, https://markets .businessinsider.com/news/stocks/warren-Buffettt-defends-propublica-tax -rate-berkshire-hathaway-stock-dvidends-2021-6-1030504042.

35. In 2024, the first $13.6 million would be free from tax, but everything over that would be taxed.

36. "Tax Expenditures Under the Estate Tax," US Department of the Treasury Office of Tax Analysis, October 20, 2016, https://home.treasury .gov/system/files/131/Tax-Expenditures-Estate-Tax-10202016.pdf.

37. "A billion here, a billion there" was often attributed to Senator Everett Dirksen, although there is no record of it. "Senator Everett McKinley Dirksen Dies," US Senate, September 7, 1969, https://www.senate.gov/artandhis tory/history/minute/Senator_Everett_Mckinley_Dirksen_Dies.htm.

38. In 2024 there was $1.5 trillion in private foundations. "Nonprofit Organizations; Total Financial Assets Held by Private Foundations, Level," FRED, https://fred.stlouisfed.org/series/BOGZ1FL164090015Q. Donoradvised funds had about $228 billion. National Philanthropic Trust, *The 2024 DAF Report*, https://www.nptrust.org/reports/daf-report/.

39. According to James Fishman: "From the earliest decades of the twentieth century private foundations were suspect organizations. They were criticized by the left as a device to allow the affluent to maintain control

of their businesses without the burdens of paying income and estate taxes and to use their wealth through the foundation form to influence politics, policy and society. Those on the right charged that private foundations were used for radical political purposes such as voter registration drives and support of civil rights." James J. Fishman, "The Private Foundation Rules at Fifty: How Did We Get Them and Do They Meet Current Needs?," *Pittsburgh Tax Review* 17, no. 2 (2020): 248, https://doi.org/10.5195/taxreview .2020.112.

40. Thomas A. Troyer, "The 1969 Private Foundation Law: Historical Perspective on Its Origins and Underpinnings," *Exempt Organization Tax Review* 27, no. 1 (2000): 52–65.

41. Lila Corwin Berman, "How Norman Sugarman Became $50B Godfather of Charitable Funds," *Forward*, November 14, 2015, https://for ward.com/news/324259/how-norman-sugarman-became-50b-godfather -of-charitable-funds/.

42. Corwin Berman, "How Norman Sugarman Became $50B Godfather of Charitable Funds."

43. Helen Flannery, "More Than Half of America's 20 Top Public Charities Are Donor-Advised Funds," Inequality.org, September 7, 2023, https:// inequality.org/article/top-public-charities/.

44. Those defending the status quo argue that DAFs do not need to have payout requirements because they already pay out at significantly higher rates than the 5 percent imposed on private foundations. However, the problem is that DAF sponsors provide only sponsor-level, not individual-DAF-level, information, and averages can hide lots of ills. We know that numerous small DAF accounts, including those provided as part of employee benefit plans, essentially act as flow-through accounts (money comes in and out within a short period). If 20 percent of the accounts operate this way, a sponsoring organization can have an overall payout rate of 20 percent, even if the remaining 80 percent stays warehoused in the DAF. Recent studies of account-level information lend support to these concerns. One such study that looked at DAFs at Michigan community foundations showed that, in 2020, a year of unprecedented need, 35 percent of DAFs did not make a single distribution to charity, and 57 percent distributed less than 5 percent of their assets. Finally, even though three-fourths of DAF sponsors had rules requiring their DAF accounts to make a distribution at least once every three years, 13 percent of DAFs made no distributions over a four-year period. J. Williams and B. Kienker, *Analysis of Donor Advised Funds from a Community Foundation Perspective*, Council of Michigan Foundations, June 2021, https://www

.michiganfoundations.org/system/files/documents/2021-09/CMFDAFRe
port_Final_6_21_2021.pdf.

45. Charitable gifts to hate groups can have devastating effects both
within and outside the United States. Proposed legislation in Uganda imposing the death penalty for homosexuals was supported by significant
charitable donations from United States taxpayers, many of which came
from donor-advised funds. Lydia Namubiro, "Charity Loophole Lets
US Donors Give Far-Right Groups $272m in Secret," Open Democracy,
July 5, 2023, https://www.opendemocracy.net/en/5050/donor-advised
-funds-daf-us-charity-law-loophole-bankroll-hate/.

46. Accelerating Charitable Efforts Act, S.1981, 117th Cong. (2021–22).

47. Bureau of Economic Analysis, *NIPA Handbook: Concepts and Methods of the US National Income and Product Accounts*, https://www.bea.gov
/resources/methodologies/nipa-handbook.

48. "Comments by Warren E. Buffett in Conjunction with His Annual
Contribution."

49. "Comments by Warren E. Buffett in Conjunction with His Annual
Contribution."

50. "The founder of Oracle says he wants to be judged on his results at
the Larry Ellison Foundation. But he must also reckon with the fact that,
for all his success in the world of making money, he has not succeeded in
the world of giving it away. He has basked in positive publicity for promises
to donate millions and then retracted offers with little explanation; sunk
hundreds of millions into moon-shot projects like life-extension research
before suddenly pulling funding; and made public promises about charitable giving that he appears nowhere close to fulfilling. Nothing has quite
worked out." Theodore Schleifer, "Larry Ellison, One of the World's Richest
People, Asks for a Second Chance at Charity," *Vox*, August 24, 2020, https://
www.vox.com/recode/2020/8/24/21369773/larry-ellison-foundation-oracle
-philanthropy. See also Theodore Schleifer, "Larry Ellison Has Abruptly
Shut Down the Foundation He Spent Years Setting Up," *Vox*, September 2, 2020, https://www.vox.com/recode/2020/9/2/21409530/larry-ellison
-foundation-disband-london-philanthropy-coronavirus.

51. Professor Miranda Perry Fleischer argues that bequests to private foundations can be tantamount to handing power down to one's heirs. Miranda
Perry Fleischer, "The Morality of Charitable Bequests," in *Inheritance and
the Right to Bequeath: Legal and Philosophical Perspectives*, ed. Hans-Christoph
Schmidt am Busch, Daniel Halliday, and Thomas Gutmann (Routledge, 2022).

52. Benjamin Soskis, "Warren Buffett's Kids Will Be the Most Powerful Philanthropists on Earth," *Town & Country*, October 29, 2024, https://

www.townandcountrymag.com/society/money-and-power/a62568250
/warren-buffett-kids-money-philanthropy/.

53. John Arnold, "Warren Buffett is leaving his $127 billion estate to a new charitable trust, whose donations must be made by unanimous agreement among his 3 kids. Meanwhile, I can't get my 3 kids to agree from which restaurant to DoorDash dinner," X, July 15, 2024, https://x.com/JohnArnoldFndtn /status/1813008091069489167.

54. Andrew Carnegie, "The Gospel of Wealth," in *The Gospel of Wealth and Other Timely Essays*, ed. Andrew C. Kirkland (1962), https://www.carn egie.org/about/our-history/gospelofwealth/.

55. This example, one of many, is posted by "Susan," "More Justice vs. Charity: Babies in the River," Compassionate San Antonio, July 17, 2022, https://sacompassion.net/more-justice-vs-charity-babies-in-the-river/.

56. Paul G. Schervish, "Hyperagency and High-Tech Donors: A New Theory of the New Philanthropists" (paper, Social Welfare Research Institute, Chestnut Hill, MA), November 14, 2003, http://hdl.handle.net/2345 /bc-ir:104107.

57. Schervish, in "Hyperagency," writes: "If agents are *finders* of the most desirable or fitting place for themselves within a limited range of possibilities, hyperagents are *founders* of those possibilities for themselves, as well as for others. What takes the aid of a social, political, religious, or philanthropic movement for agents to achieve, can be achieved by hyperagents pretty much single-handedly" (2).

58. Matthew Bishop and Michael Green, *Philanthrocapitalism: How the Rich Can Save the World* (Bloomsbury Press, 2008), 12.

59. Gary Baum, "Brad Pitt and the Bizarre Charity Mess That's Left Katrina Victims Stranded Again," *Hollywood Reporter*, April 12, 2023, https://www .hollywoodreporter.com/business/business-news/brad-pitt-charity-mess -katrina-victims-stranded-1235371222/; Wilfred Chan, "Brad Pitt Foundation Agrees on $20.5M Settlement to Owners of Faulty Post-Katrina Houses," *The Guardian*, August 18, 2022, https://www.theguardian.com/us-news /2022/aug/17/brad-pitt-foundation-settlement-owners-faulty-post-katrina -houses.

60. Valerie Strauss, "Bill and Melinda Gates Have Spent Billions to Shape Education Policy. Now, They Say, They're 'Skeptical' of 'Billionaires' Trying to Do Just That," *Washington Post*, February 10, 2020, https://www .washingtonpost.com/education/2020/02/10/bill-melinda-gates-have-spent -billions-dollars-shape-education-policy-now-they-say-theyre-skeptical-bil lionaires-trying-do-just-that/. See, e.g., Brian M. Stecher, Deborah J. Holtzman, Michael S. Garet, et al., *Improving Teaching Effectiveness: Final*

Report, RAND, June 21, 2018, https://www.rand.org/pubs/research_reports /RR2242.html.

61. Edwin Black, *War Against the Weak* (Dialog Press, 2012), 14.

62. "Galton himself was forced to admit . . . that his theories and formulae were still completely unprovable." Black at 18. As historian Edwin Black wrote: America was ready for eugenics before eugenics was ready for America. Black, *War Against the Weak*, 21.

63. Black, *War Against the Weak*, 38.

64. Black, *War Against the Weak*; William A. Schambra, "Philanthropy's Original Sin," *New Atlantis*, Summer 2013, https://www.thenewatlantis.com /publications/philanthropys-original-sin.

65. Eric D. Isaacs, "Statement on Eugenics Research," Carnegie Science, August 12, 2020, https://carnegiescience.edu/about/history/statement -eugenics-research; William A. Schambra, "Carnegie's Midnight Confession," Hudson Institute, January 12, 2021, https://www.hudson.org/human-rights /carnegie-s-midnight-confession.

CHAPTER SIX

1. M. J. Lee, "Buffett's Secretary Speaks," *Politico*, January 26, 2012, https:// www.politico.com/story/2012/01/buffett-secty-fairness-for-avg-citizens -071998.

2. Jesse Eisinger, Jeff Ernsthausen, and Paul Kiel, "The Secret IRS Files: Trove of Never-Before-Seen Records Reveal How the Wealthiest Avoid Income Tax," ProPublica, June 8, 2021, https://www.propublica.org /article/the-secret-irs-files-trove-of-never-before-seen-records-reveal-how -the-wealthiest-avoid-income-tax.

3. Alexis de Tocqueville, *The Old Regime and the Revolution (1856)*, trans George Gerald Reisman, 113, available at https://oll.libertyfund.org/titles /tocqueville-the-old-regime-and-the-revolution-1856.

4. See generally Sidney Ratner, *Taxation and Democracy in America* (John Wiley & Sons, 1967). For additional sources on the phenomenon of tax reform as a means of undercutting radical revolutionary action from across the political spectrum, see Joseph J. Thorndike, "News Analysis: Can Taxes Prevent Social Unrest?," *TaxNotes*, January 3, 2012, https://www .taxnotes.com/tax-history-project/news-analysis-can-taxes-prevent-social -unrest/2012/01/03/vc0c; Seymour Martin Lipset and Gary Marks, "How FDR Saved Capitalism," *Hoover Institute*, January 30, 2001, https://www .hoover.org/research/how-fdr-saved-capitalism.

5. Molly Berger, "The Rich Man's City: Hotels and Mansions of Gilded Age New York," *Journal of Decorative and Propaganda Arts* 25 (January 2005): 61.

6. Michael McGerr, *A Fierce Discontent: The Rise and Fall of the Progressive Movement in America* (Oxford University Press, 2005), 245, 256–57; "Some New York Palaces," *Harper's Weekly*, April 7, 1894; John Tauranac, *Elegant New York: The Builders and the Buildings* (Abbeville Press, 1985), 116; "The Vanderbilt Palaces," *New York Times*, August 25, 1881, 3; "The Vanderbilt Houses," *Harper's Weekly* January 21, 1882, 42.

7. Berger, "Rich Man's City," 57–58; Thorstein Veblen, *The Theory of the Leisure Class* (Vanguard Press, 1912), 38.

8. Himadri Roy Chaudhuri and Sitanath Majumdar, "Of Diamonds and Desires: Understanding Conspicuous Consumption from a Contemporary Marketing Perspective," *Academy of Marketing Science Review* 10 (January 2006): 5.

9. Robert Armstrong and Lauren Indvik, "How to Look Rich," *Financial Times*, October 3, 2023, https://www.ft.com/content/8dc9d813 -e658-4f2e-bb64-9fa5a0820fd6.

10. Jethro Mullen and Daniel Shane, "Weed, Whiskey, Tesla and a Flame-thrower: Elon Musk Meets Joe Rogan," *CNN*, October 1, 2018, https://www .cnn.com/2018/10/01/tech/elon-musk-joe-rogan/index.html.

11. Michael Mechanic, "How the 1 Percent Lives," *Monterey County Now*, June 4, 2021, https://www.montereycountynow.com/news/cover/a-deep -dive-into-the-reality-of-the-super-rich-and-how-wealth-molds-how/article _d0425260-c3de-11eb-b58d-03d45fdc2b2b.html.

12. A 2013 study found that the percentage of families living in either "poor" neighborhoods or their "affluent" counterparts has more than doubled from 1970 to 2012. In the same period, "middle" neighborhoods, those where the median income is between 80 percent and 125 percent of the regional median, have shrunk from containing 65 percent of all American families to a paltry 42 percent. Alan Mallach, "Is the Urban Middle Neighborhood an Endangered Species? Multiple Challenges and Difficult Answers," *Community Development Innovation Review* 11, no. 1 (August 2016): 52.

13. Claudia Goldin and Robert A. Margo, "The Great Compression: The Wage Structure in the United States at Mid-Century," *Quarterly Journal of Economics* 107, no. 1 (February 1992): 1–34; William J. Collins and Gregory Niemesh, "Income Gains and the Geography of the US Home Ownership Boom, 1940 to 1960," *National Bureau of Economic Research* (May 2024): https://doi.org/10.3386/w31249; Sam Pizzigati, "The Two Decades That Created Our World's First Mass Middle Class," *Inequality.org*, May 18,

2023, https://inequality.org/great-divide/the-two-decades-that-created-our
-worlds-first-mass-middle-class/; "Homeownership-Past, Present, and Future," *U.S. Housing Market Conditions Summary* (Summer 1994), https://www
.huduser.gov/periodicals/ushmc/summer94/summer94.html.

14. Michael McGerr, "Progressivism, Liberalism and the Rich," in *The Progressives Century: Political Reform, Constitutional Government and the Modern American State*, ed. Stephen Skowronek, Stephen M. Engel, and Bruce Ackerman (Yale University Press 2016), 252; Kevin Phillips, *Wealth and Democracy* (Broadway Books, 2002), 68–82.

15. Juliana Kaplan, "To Feel Middle Class, You Have to Be Wealthy," *Business Insider*, May 18, 2024, https://www.businessinsider.com/what-it
-takes-to-be-middle-class-middle-income-wealth-2024-5.

16. "Housing Wealth Gains for the Rising Middle-Class Markets," National Association of Realtors, 2022, https://www.nar.realtor/research-and-statistics
/research-reports/housing-wealth-gains-for-the-rising-middle-class-markets; Andrew Van Dam, "How Inheritance Data Secretly Explains U.S. Inequality," *Washington Post*, November 10, 2023, https://www.washingtonpost.com
/business/2023/11/10/inheritance-america-taxes-equality/; Pascale Bourquin, Robert Joyce, and David Sturrock, "Inherited Wealth on Course to be a Much More Important Determinant of Lifetime Resources for Today's Young Than It Was for Previous Generations," Institute for Fiscal Studies, July 22, 2020, https://ifs.org.uk/articles/inherited-wealth-course-be-much
-more-important-determinant-lifetime-resources-todays-young.

17. Bourquin et al., "Inherited Wealth."

18. "The Estate Tax Is Irrelevant to More Than 99 Percent of Americans," Institute on Taxation and Economic Policy, December 7, 2023, https://itep
.org/federal-estate-tax-historic-lows-2023.

19. "Income Tax Returns as Made Public Here Show Many Big Payments, One Above Million," *New York Times*, October 24, 1924, https://timesmachine
.nytimes.com/timesmachine/1924/10/24/104266293.html?pageNumber=1. Some have advocated for bringing back this type of publicity to promote transparency and discourage tax evasion. See Binyamin Appelbaum, "Everyone's Income Taxes Should Be Public," *New York Times*, April 13, 2019, https://www.nytimes.com/2019/04/13/opinion/sunday/taxe as-public.html.

20. Eisinger et al., "The Secret IRS Files."

21. Erica York, "Summary of the Latest Federal Income Tax Data, 2025 Update," Tax Foundation, November 18, 2024, https://taxfoundation.org
/data/all/federal/latest-federal-income-tax-data-2025/.

22. Internal Revenue Code, 26 U.S.C. § 61.

23. Internal Revenue Code, 26 U.S.C. § 104.

24. See, among others, Lily Batchelder, "Taxing Privilege More Effectively: Replacing the Estate Tax with an Inheritance Tax," Hamilton Project, June 1, 2007, https://www.hamiltonproject.org/publication/policy-proposal/taxing-privilege-more-effectively-replacing-the-estate-tax-with-an-inheritance-tax/; Joseph M. Dodge, "Replacing the Estate Tax with a Re-Imagined Accessions Tax" (Public Law Research Paper No. 325, FSU College of Law), October 16, 2008, https://papers.ssrn.com/sol3/papers.cfm?abstract_id=1285515; Samuel D. Brunson, "Afterlife of the Death Tax," *Indiana Law Journal* 94, no. 2 (2019): Article 1, https://www.repository.law.indiana.edu/ilj/vol94/iss2/1/.

25. See Batchelder, "Taxing Privilege More Effectively."

26. While the double-tax argument is often employed, much of the wealth captured by the estate tax is on unrealized gains, which are not taxed under the income tax. In fact, recent research has suggested that as much as 44 percent of the wealth captured by the current regime is unrealized gains, with larger estates generally having a higher ratio of wealth untaxed outside of the estate tax system. Jane G. Gravelle, *The Estate and Gift Tax: An Overview*, Congressional Research Service, September 16, 2024, https://crsreports.congress.gov/product/pdf/R/R48183. See also Chuck Marr and Samantha Jacoby, "Arguments Against Taxing Unrealized Capital Gains of Very Wealthy Fall Flat," Center on Budget and Policy Priorities, September 11, 2024, https://www.cbpp.org/research/federal-tax/arguments-against-taxing-unrealized-capital-gains-of-very-wealthy-fall-flat.

27. James R. Repetti, "Democracy, Taxes and Wealth," *NYU Law Review* 76 (2001): 825–73, at 850.

28. While Canada has no estate tax, President Nixon and President Obama both proposed retaining the estate tax and adopting realization at death.

29. William G. Gale, Oliver Hall, and John Sabelhaus, "Taxing the 'Angel of Death,'" Brookings Institution, January 23, 2025, https://www.brookings.edu/articles/taxing-the-angel-of-death/.

30. See ACTEC, "Deemed Realization of Gains on Gratuitous Transfers," *ACTEC Trust & Estate Talk* (podcast), episode 82, November 2019, https://actecfoundation.org/podcasts/deemed-realization-tax/.

31. Tocqueville, *Old Regime and the Revolution*, 113.

Index